Ivan Antic

SAMADHI

Unity of Consciousness and Existence

SAMKHYA PUBLISHING LTD
London, 2020

Translated by
Milica Breber

Proofreading & editing by
James Joshua Pennington, PhD

Copyright © 2020 by SAMKHYA PUBLISHING LTD
All rights reserved.
ISBN: 978-1986066075

Dedicated to Doinita Lapadat
(1943 – 2016)
In maha-samadhi
With love

Table of Contents

Introduction...	7
The Nature of Existence...............................	12
The Nature of Energy	17
It is Not Matter that Fluctuates, but Information Everything is Momentary and Nothing is Substantial	21
There is No Multitude of Particles: Everything is Only One, Divine Particle	23
Parallel Realities	29
The Dimensions of Existence	36
Humans are a Microcosm Comprised of All the Dimensions of Nature	40
The Nature of Consciousness...........................	46
The Soul's Consciousness and its Incarnation into the Body Through the Higher Mind	49
Unity of Consciousness and Existence, of Body and Soul...	59
If Everything is a Reflection of the Divine Consciousness, Why is There Evil in the World?	67
The Law of Number Seven and the Seven Chakras	86
The Division of Chakras into Three Sections	91
The Hertzian and Non Hertzian Frequencies of Chakras	96
Polarization of Opposites in Chakras	102
The Higher and Lower Nature of Chakras	105
The Fundamental Nature and the Meaning of Every Chakra	111
The Principle of Chakra Functioning in the World and Historical Development	129
Examples of Chakra Functioning in the History of Spirituality	131
Examples of Chakra Functioning in the Personal Development of Humans	133
The Energetic Chakra Activation........................	139

Physical Exercises for Harmonious Chakra Activation 145
The Exercise of Imagination and Breathing for Chakra Activation... 148
The Principle of Energy Preservation for the Sublimation of Consciousness 150
The Basic Principles of Sublimating Consciousness Through Chakras 155
Samadhi – The Unity of Consciousness and Existence 169

INTRODUCTION

Existence and the awareness of existence make up the entirety of being – beyond this, there is nothing. At the base they are one; however, they are expressed as though they are separate. The relationship between consciousness and existence creates all of nature, including the cosmos. Our mind is only an instrument that, like a prism, refracts the unique light of consciousness into the full spectrum of existence. Outside of our mind, existence and consciousness are one.

The relationship between consciousness and existence is at the base of everything– all phenomena, matter and events – which is most clearly illuminated by and through human beings. Consciousness and existence are differentiated in humans to achieve their fullest potential, realized as supreme awareness. Therefore, we may conclude that the human essence is to fully realize this relationship between consciousness and existence, to implement and understand it, and to bear this burden. Human essence is determined by the relationship towards existence; more accurately, towards the essence of Being.[1] Outwardly, this relationship is demonstrated by the progress of civilization, culture and technology. Within humans, this connection between existence and consciousness is manifested most dominantly in the form of language and thought development, and, in its

---

[1] This is how Martin Heidegger defined the essence of philosophy. See interview: Martin Heidegger Talks Philosophy with a Buddhist Monk on German Television (1963).

final outcome, as knowledge of the self and God, or enlightenment.

Therefore, existence and consciousness are essentially one and the same, even though they are manifested as opposites – one as existence and the other as the awareness of that existence. Existence is conditioned by its own causality, while consciousness is unconditioned. Existence is simply everything that exists, in any possible permutation, and consciousness is akin to the space that enables the existence of everything. In this way, consciousness is always superior to any form of existence and profoundly independent of everything – it is transcendental. Only thanks to its transcendental essence does consciousness enable the realization of absolutely everything that exists. ***The fact that consciousness transcends existence makes the objective awareness of existence possible. The possibility for transcendence is the essence of consciousness.***

Humans are the link between existence and consciousness which enables this existence. He is the connecting factor. All other beings simply exist, with varying degrees of complexity, but always conditioned by spontaneous causality, which requires no such awareness. Only man possesses the objective awareness of existence in all its shapes and possibilities, awareness of the entirety of nature, and therefore an objective awareness of himself. The symbolism of the cross best depicts the relationship between existence and consciousness. The horizontal axis denotes existence in time, and the vertical axis represents the surpassing or transcendence of such an existence by means of a vertical change in awareness and comprehension, together with the surpassing of time and causality. It is a cross that every man must shoulder in this world. In its essence, it is the differentiation of consciousness, or more accurately, the true distinction of what consciousness actually is. Finally, it can be said that **the very differentiation** of consciousness and existence constitutes both consciousness and existence.

The merging of consciousness and existence culminates in the very act of comprehending that very existence, the foundation for both the mind and creativity. Every time we make something new, we are connecting our consciousness to this existence. That is how all spiritual and material culture came into being; civilization is the consequence of uniting consciousness and existence in humans.

Our mind acts based on perception, and perception is there to discover true reality. We constantly attempt to crack open reality with everything we perceive, with everything that takes place around us, and within us as well. Discovering the facts of life is actually the act of connecting consciousness with existence.

More accurately, the idea here is that man can have objective awareness of himself. It's not guaranteed; nor is it a birthright. Human development is predestined to elevate itself to an increasingly elevated level of consciousness of existence in all aspects; all the activities humans undertake and all of their experiences present the full spectrum of all potential states that they may encounter, ranging from basic existence to an objective awareness of existence. Some are closer to existence and further away from consciousness, and for this reason they are more unconscious, while others are closer to consciousness and more distant from the blinding conditioning influence of existence. Differences in the level of consciousness between people (the ratio between consciousness and existence) are evinced by the variable dramatics of life, the variety of human characters, and the range in developmental progress of differing cultures. The more alert people are, the more they are in harmony with understanding and love; the more unconscious they are, the more conditioned they are by natural causality, suffering from an inner conflict with nature, the world, and the people around them.

Since human essence is determined by the extent of consciousness of existence, it is essence is equally transcendent to the essence of consciousness. If this were not the case, humans would not be able to unite existence and consciousness. Humans both connects and separates existence and consciousness. From the simple fact of being above both of them, they can perceive them both. They cannot experience the merging of consciousness and existence without first experiencing their separation. When a human is aware of not only existence, and not only of consciousness of that existence, but of themselves as the central element binding the two, then they are fully enlightened or realized their transcendental essence.

One such teaching that best encapsulates man's essence as described above is the teaching of *samkhya*..[2]

The only practice based on the teaching of *samkhya* and which merges consciousness and existence is the teaching of *Yoga Sutras*.[3] The term for joining consciousness with existence here is samadhi. The Sanskrit word *samadhi* literally means "joining together" or "focus". Patanjali defined samadhi as the unity of the subject and the object of perception - the consciousness of unity, or

---

[2] More on this can be found in my book: "*Samkhya - The Ancient Science of Nature and the Soul of Man*".

[3] In order to properly understand Patanjali it is necessary to get acquainted with the modern approach of Yoga Sutras as presented in "*Yoga: The Alpha and the Omega*" by Osho. The best comments on Patanjali's *Yoga Sutras* are in this text.

the transcendental consciousness, which surpasses the division of subject-object.

The completely realized unity of consciousness and existence in humans is samadhi.

We shall contribute here to this unity by describing it in detail, as it happens both inwardly and outwardly in humans themselves.

THE NATURE OF EXISTENCE

Simply put, existence is everything that exists, in any permutation. Even existence itself is an existing entity. Non-existence is impossible. Existence is absolute. In its essence, it is like the space which enables the existence of everything else, the cosmos. Every form of existence must take place within the confines of the space that enables it, while, simultaneously, space itself is unconditioned by any form of existence. Therefore, it can be said that existence splits itself into space which further enables the existence of everything that is shaped within this space. This division is, however, ostensible. The nature of our own perception forces us to view things in this way. **Only space is the unconditioned wholeness, which keeps shaping itself into a distinct existence.** Everything that exists in a distinct form is space that has shaped itself, momentarily, into that form.

Therefore, the actuality of every form of existence - of all beings, objects and phenomena - is in the present moment only. It is instantaneous, happening here and now. Everything exists solely as the current shaping of space into a specific form. Beings or objects do not exist of their own accord, as distinct and independent (substantial) phenomena, but as the current modification of the unconditioned wholeness or space.

Everything is current and interconnected in unity and wholeness.

At the beginning of the twentieth century, quantum physics discovered that our material reality is, in essence, a field of pure energy. This energy field was named the quantum field, or the universal field. It was discovered that the quantum field exists and functions as the field in which everything we see in this rough material world already exists. The quantum field serves as the hidden or implicit order behind the open or explicit world we live in.[4] All the possibilities due to manifest themselves in the visible world, in accordance with existing circumstances (like some shape or phenomenon), are already there, and consequently, all the events of life are already there ready to come to fruition (predetermined).

In accordance with this, the nature of reality is always one and the same, but it exists dually: as both hidden and as manifested. When it is unmanifested it resides in its quantum field of pure energy, but when manifested it is present in some rough form or as an event. Because of this, nothing is new in the universe, it merely appears so to our perception, as something that is manifesting before our eyes and originating from the quantum field of multiple possibilities. But everything that has manifested itself was already present in its potential form. Nothing can come from nothing. Everything has its cause. The origin of all causes is the universal quantum field. Traditionally, this was identified in esoteric philosophy as the ether, or *akasha* in Sanskrit.

Akasha translates to "space".

This is why we have stated that only existence exists, and that non-existence is impossible. Existence is absolute: we ourselves, every thought, experience, every deed, every fact and every event in the cosmos have always existed, and will always exist; more accurately, they exist timelessly. They are all nothing but the modifica-

---

[4] David Bohm, "Wholeness and the Implicate Order" (First published 1980 by Routledge & Kegan Paul)

tions of space, and nothing outside of this is possible. Our life experience consists of singling out a detail from this wholeness of existence in time and space. This singling out is the differentiation of consciousness from existence, or more precisely, differential ontology.

It has been experimentally proven that the subatomic world acts irrelevant of time and space, and that everything within it is interconnected. Information for all subatomic particles is transmitted instantaneously, although the particles are (seemingly) separate in space. In other words, in this quantum field, the rudimentary field of reality, everything is interconnected in a unified network. Nature, in its most basic form, is one unique Whole, without any divisions.

In accordance with this, it has been discovered that the nature of reality corresponds to that of the holograph. This is the origin of the theory of the holographic universe, which explains that everything in the cosmos is interconnected in a way similar to a holograph: where every tiny bit contains an image of the whole.[5]

This is of key importance for comprehending consciousness, because in the final outcome, it appears that consciousness is the basis for all of nature. Every particle and every atom have immediate communication with all of the other particles across the entire universe. The whole cosmos is one big information system that communicates instantaneously across all of its seemingly di-

---

[5] On the universal field in modern physics see: "The Field: The Quest for the Secret Force of the Universe" by Lynne McTaggart (2003). On the holographic paradigm see: "The Holographic Universe" by Michael Talbot (1991). On understanding and connecting consciousness and the quantum field with the holographic universe, see: "The Divine Matrix: Bridging Time, Space, Miracles, and Belief" by Gregg Braden (2006).

vided parts. Aside from being a characteristic of the most profound form of attachment, communication is the basic property of consciousness. Holographic unity of the universe enables instantaneous communication and that is one of the characteristics of the consciousness. This is a more complex illustration for the purpose of revealing how consciousness is connected with existence.

Our nervous system exists, in its entirety, as the mechanism which slows down instant pieces of communication, like a filter which disables the instantaneous flow of information of all existence trying to reach our perception. Our brain, together with the nervous system, serves only to slow down the functioning of nature to below the speed of light in linear time. Our nervous system does not create or convey consciousness, it only slows consciousness down to a recognizable level, in order for us to be able to communicate and live in this three-dimensional physical reality in the way we exist now. If it were not so, we would be lost in the entirety of nature, and it would not be possible for us to exist in this physical form.

For the same reason, when the cerebral functions of the nervous system are disabled, we experience higher states of consciousness, higher dimensions, and the physical world appears to us like something we see in a dream because we reside in it with a very limited consciousness. However, such a nervous system does not restrict our functioning completely, because our consciousness is far bigger than our nervous system. If we reduced ourselves to utilizing the nervous system only, we would be hardened materialists, and our perception level would be on par with that of animals. This is not the case with all people. There is the possibility of utilizing far greater consciousness to alter our reality and our environment. Our consciousness is, in its essence, the same consciousness that implements the quantum field. The higher aptitudes of our consciousness are called, by some, the divine consciousness; or it is defined as our link to God. Others have called it the quantum mind or thinking, the "quantum consciousness". Here we shall refer to it simply as consciousness or the soul's consciousness, but we emphasize that our soul is an individual expression of the divine consciousness that enables everything, including existence itself.

THE NATURE OF ENERGY

If energy is at the core of everything, the obvious question becomes: What is energy? The word itself derives from the Greek *energeia* meaning "activity, action, operation", parsed as en, a preposition meaning "in, at", plus the noun *ergon* 'work' (from Proto-Indo-European *werg-, from whence English work derives). Therefore, energy equals work, and in some sense creation because only motion can transform an idea into a concrete shape or phenomenon. In other words, this motion is a vibration that enables an idea to manifest. The essence of any motion is vibration, based on electromagnetic polarization.[6]

Polarization generates the movement of everything, from an electron to gravity. This movement is energy, perpetually manifesting itself through some function or motion. Energy is vibration, and the most fundamental vibration of nature is that of the vibrating quantum field. It solely consists of vibrations. For this reason, it is said that it is a field of pure energy, and the source of

---

[6] The original Greek denotes energy as every movement which happens in existence, in being, because movement alone is energy. Since everything is in motion, then everything can be seen as energy. Nowadays, even our language has devalued the view of existence as energy; we see everything as "dead matter" and energy is only what we produce by means of combustion or electricity. In the modern world, only quantum physics and mysticism remind us that matter does not exist, and that everything in its purest sense is just energy. Chakras show us the connection between the consciousness and energy in us; more accurately, they reflect all the aspects of the functioning of consciousness.

all the energy there is (the infinite energy of the zero point, dark matter). These vibrations are also called the quantum fluctuation.

According to the model of fractal geometry, the initial subtle differences in vibrations (otherwise known as the quantum fluctuation) come gradually bigger and more complex energy vibrations – namely, various vibratory-energetic structures and constructions. Furthermore, even more complex forms are manifested as particles on the crude level, and as clusters of particles and atoms that attract or repel each other in accordance with the nature of their vibrations, thus creating bigger forms such as molecules, right up until the moment when a group of molecules forms what we recognize as a physical form, a being, phenomenon or event.

All things and all phenomena come into being according to this model, from the most subtle energy vibrations of the quantum field to the crude physical world we perceive with our senses. For this reason, we say that everything is energy. When we stated above that everything is only space shaping itself into distinct forms, we noted that everything is just *akasha*, the quantum field, that exists only as energy which shapes itself by means of various frequencies expressing themselves into versatile phenomena. Therefore, all the differences we perceive here, for example between metal and plastic, are basically just differences in vibrations on the subatomic level; the particles that make metal vibrate one way, and plastic another. That's it. There are no differences in the material because nothing is material, everything is just energy that vibrates in a different way.

And yet there's more to say about energy. Its essence can be explained as follows.

If energy (a being in action) is in its essence a quantum field which is timeless, *energy is everything that takes place in the cosmos, and everything that possibly could be; energy is the compressed action of everything, the most subtle expression of that action, because it is the very nature of the quantum field itself.* Energy, in its quantum essence, is the potential (information) of any kind of phenomenon, none of which is possible without energy. Energy of the quantum field and all the motion and action in the cosmos are one and the same, however, since it occurs in different proportions and dimensions, *in the outside world all energy appears to be crude matter or events in the world, while in its most refined state in the quantum field, it remains as pure energy potential (information).*

Existence removes place from time completely; i.e. there is no time in the essence of existence. Therefore, energy for all actions can be manifested in existence during the course of time; it can revert to itself, while it is still in existence in the quantum field. The ultimate goal of existence - the energy of the quantum field - can always reach every act of existence in space and time. It does so invariably. The timeless quantum field perpetually expressing itself as a versatile existence in space and time. That is why there is energy in existence everywhere, and why it is not separate from existence. This is a consequence of the independence of the quantum field from time. In its rough expression, energy is somewhat restricted by its purpose and the form of action, but it always maintains its original quantum nature; otherwise it would not be energy.

Energy is the finest form of action, the information for the action. The starting quantum form of energy and the final outcome in the form of a phenomenon are one and the same, because there is no time in the essence of existence. *In this manner, existence grants itself the energy for all its manifestations. Owing to the relativity of time, there is no outside source of energy for everything that takes place in the cosmos.*

IT IS NOT MATTER THAT FLUCTUATES BUT INFORMATION
Everything is Momentary and Nothing is Substantial

If energy at its very core is motion, then we'll need a proper definition of motion. Motion is simply information that moves. A wave is synchronized oscillation that in turn stimulates another wave. It is not solid matter that is transferred by the wave, like a particle through space, but simply information that initiates the next corresponding information. All crude forms have their origin in subtle information. Take a tidal wave, for example, which is not water itself moving on top of the ocean surface, as it may appear, but instead as a sequence of oscillations moving through the water. In this way, nothing is substantial, there is no matter that moves through time and space. All shapes are actually the current state of vibrations of space, *akasha*, or the quantum field. Everything exists according to this principal of momentariness.

This is the method by which space can modify itself into any shape. We have already stated that there are no separate objects in space, but rather there is space alone that in an instant can modify itself into any shape. It is clear now that this is another way of stating that space, which is *akasha* or the quantum field, with its vibrations, provides energy and shape to every form of existence which we, due to our own limited perception, detect as separate shapes appearing in space. Furthermore, it is now even clearer to us that every vibration is actually a piece of information.

Information is the essence of energy and shapes, because consciousness is at the base of the modification of information.

Consciousness is at the foundation of everything.

THERE IS NO MULTITUDE OF PARTICLES:
Everything is Only One, Divine Particle

In order to comprehend the nature of existence, it's not sufficient to say that it's based on the energy of the quantum field, or that its arranged according to the model of the holograph, or that it is current. It is imperative that we explain why existence is the way it is. Only then will we be able to understand why consciousness is the foundation of all existence.

Namely, consciousness is no different than existence itself. Otherwise, there would be no awareness of existence, and no self-consciousness of man. Therefore, the nature of existence cannot be separated from the nature of consciousness, or the consciousness of existence itself, and existence and consciousness of existence cannot be separated from the self-consciousness of man.

In an attempt to analyze the consciousness of existence, we use the most basic logic in order to understand the concept of existence. Existence is always something that exists, as the foundation of everything that exists, something which is perpetual and absolute. Everything that exists must possess some wider grounds on which to reside, some cause; the widest concept which enables everything to exist is the Absolute (or the Being in Platonic philosophy). His definition is completeness; nothing is possible outside it or without it. The state of being unconditioned, the Absolute is also the freedom that enables everything else. Therefore, the Absolute has divine properties. It has the characteristic of space, or is the one that enables space itself which, in turn, enables everything that can exist to exist.

Although the Absolute has no individual traits, the quality of spaciousness is the closest we can get in our effort to conceive it. Therefore, let us imagine the divine Absolute as the empty space in which there is absolutely nothing. As such it is unmanifested, unexpressed and unaware of its true potential. This state is very close to the experience of non-existence. However, non-existence is an impossibility, by definition. This creates an existential paradox. If the divine Absolute remains unmanifested, it will remain so in the form of nothing or emptiness, but nothing or emptiness cannot exist. This paradox creates tension within the divine Absolute and forces it to express itself and manifest, which, at the same time, is the act of bringing itself into full awareness of itself and the awareness of its full potential. **Hence, the Absolute as everything-that-is, manifests itself into everything-that-can-be.** This is the fundamental principle of existence.

For this reason, the divine Absolute manifests itself in the simplest way possible, **directly, as its own opposition**. No other option is possible. The opposite of sheer endless space in which there is absolutely nothing, contrary to the void, is one single particle. We shall appropriately name it "the divine particle" – with no religious connotations intended. It was infinitely small, and had overwhelming infinite potential. It had to be like this to act as the opposition to the infinitely big and infinitely empty space. 'The divine particle' we are dealing with here is basically just the virtual opposite to the unconditioned void of the divine Absolute; it is no different from the Absolute, it is only the Absolute's imagination used to express itself and all its possibilities. It possesses no mass and nothing can affect it. It is as unconditioned as the divine Absolute itself.

A similar idea was concocted by the founder of elementary logical deduction in three dimensions, Euclid, in his work 'Elements'. Euclid's geometry is based not on an ordinary mathematical system but as a mathematical formulation of Plato's philosophy of ideas. Euclid defines a point as 'that which has no parts', otherwise understood as the occult definition of the Being that is otherwise called the Absolute. According to that definition, the Being, the Absolute, is 'that which has no parts'. In this way, one point is geometrically the notion of eternity or the whole, the Absolute. The point is a non-spatial entity; it is unimaginable for space to have no dimensions and therefore, this definition of the point coincides with the metaphysical notion of the Being or the divine Absolute.

The point is also the basis for orientation in space, the first phenomenon of existence. In this way, when the Absolute manifests itself through its opposition, the point, the base for every objective existence, emerges.

Likewise, this is the same singular point which in the fancy of physicists existed before the alleged 'Big Bang'.

Cosmologists, thinking according to their materialistic minds, developed the theory that this "divine particle" "exploded into the 'Big Bang' that later created the entire cosmos and all the elements, and that the cosmos keeps expanding due to this explosion, and will also, in the long run, reach the point of the 'Big Crunch', when the full brunt of the explosion wears out. They assert that this singular point created a multitude of subatomic particles, a multitude of atoms and molecules, and all the material universe which creates even more complex structures as a result of mutual reactions.

However, enlightened people who see reality the way it really is, say one and the same thing: nothing outside the divine Absolute can exist, and the Absolute perpetually manifests itself into everything that can possibly exist; its manifestation is the awareness of existence, and its consciousness is the same consciousness with which we are aware of ourselves. In fact, they say there is no multitude but only unity, that God or the Absolute was never lost but is ever-present, the one that is here and now, in everything, as everything-that-is.

What really happened with that point, or 'the divine particle," if it did not explode in the 'Big Bang'?

Nothing happened to it, it is just important to understand its nature.

In contrast to the Absolute itself, while at the same time being in the Absolute, the point has all the capacity within itself, just as the Absolute does. It can, as experiments with subatomic particles have shown, reside in two or more places simultaneously; it can act as a particle or an energy wave, and all its shapes are interconnected in non-local communication. In other words: creation is current and absolute, never linear. This 'divine particle' has properties and speeds far greater than the speed of light, and it can manifest itself and appear in several places simultaneously; **in reality, it manifests itself and acts in all possible places simultaneously.**

And it does so, continuously and currently, meaning simultaneously, by manifesting itself in all possible shapes; it cannot stand still because its very purpose is to be a reflection of all of the potentials of the divine Absolute. Since the Absolute cannot exist in time and space, its virtual particle does not need time to manifest itself either, and it is not conditioned by space. For this reason, it is far quicker than the speed of light; in short – it is instantaneous.

Its concurrent appearance in many places, looks to an insufficiently aware observer, like humans with a weaker consciousness, as though there were multiple particles, as though they created a myriad of various atoms and elements, objects in space and time. It only seems to be this way because its speed exceeds the speed of the mind and the perception of light; its speed is instantaneous. The entire illusion of the multitude of elements and objects the cosmos is filled with is created by this single 'divine particle,' due to its speed and its characteristic to reflect (like a mirror) all the possibilities of the divine Absolute, instantly. In the same way a painter paints many paintings with the colors and shapes and only one brush, the divine Absolute does the same with only one particle, which is not a particle in the typical sense of the word, but rather an instant reflection of the divine Absolute in all its detail and potential.

There is no multitude. This is the final truth behind all stories of unity, of everything being connected to One, and of everything being connected to God. This is the background of the Buddhist teaching on the immediateness of creation - the only objective teaching of the nature of reality; it is the foundation of *advaita vedanta*, which speaks of the non-existence of duality in nature.

It is the basic reason why consciousness is ever present in the entire existence, why all beings are the result of a conscious, intelligent design, and not some slow evolutionary process; it is possible only due to the momentariness of existence itself. If existence were substantial, if time existed as a linear phenomenon, consciousness would need to go on a very long journey and burn a lot of fuel in the process. The current existence of everything in the form of a single particle explains how consciousness and energy are inherent in existence itself.[7]

---

[7] The phrase we use here, 'the divine particle', has nothing in common with book: "The God Particle" a 1993 popular science book by Leon M. Lederman and Dick Teresi. This book is mainstream science. Here 'the divine particle' is like a point in Euclid's geometry, which has no dimensional properties, but it has all the properties of the Absolute.

PARALLEL REALITIES

Reality is made up of all the potential realities that exist in parallel, here and now.

In the very essence of existence there is no time and everything takes place by means of instant manifestation of the 'divine particle' within the holographic universe. There is nothing new because everything that has manifested itself in existence already existed in the universal quantum field as a possibility.

Every motion of the Being is successively transforming space from one current state to another; there is no movement of the Being itself through space. There are no beings that move through space, but space (*akasha*, the quantum field) instantly and successively shape itself in such a way, on this rough plain that our senses are able to perceive, that it seems like an object is moving through space. The same applies for the reality in which we currently reside. All the realities already exist simultaneously or, better yet, timelessly. With our state of consciousness, as the supreme attractor, we induce a certain reality to manifest before us; more precisely, we choose to reside in a certain reality.

It is not outside of us and our reality, somewhere objectively far and away, it is always here and now, together with all potential realities. With our state of consciousness we have only activated one specific reality to domineer over us and our environment. It will remain dominant for as long as our state of our mind dictates. With a change in the state of consciousness, we change our reality by shifting into another, which begins to correspond to the new state of consciousness. In the same way that objects going through space do not exist, the objective transformation of one same reality does not exist, but instead the state of consciousness activates the transition from one potential reality to another.

Any change in circumstances and material states is not an outer change, as nothing ever changes on the outside - life does not function that way. Instead, one parallel reality is swapped for another. When our life changes, we have simply crossed over from one reality to another, from one frequency to another, from one state to another; we have not changed our life as if it were an object prone to change. With our state of consciousness, we have crossed over from one of the possible simultaneously existing realities to another, and to our mind, tied to a body and limited senses, this change appears like an outer change within a single reality.

Therefore, if we wish to change something in our life, we should not imagine the desired reality is somewhere far away or in the future, and that we have to attract it. It is already here, but we are not able to perceive it with our consciousness. Instead, we perceive the reality which is present and which we wish to escape. Every experience, every thought, every object and every life we can have is here and now (potentially present in the quantum field), but we do not see it and we do not experience it, it is not our reality because we are not in tune with its frequency. It will become visible and real for us only when we change ourselves, our state of consciousness, in accordance with reality. In this way, nothing comes from the outside, everything is here and now, the only real factor is the conscious subject of objective events - we ourselves - and our state of consciousness. This determines and activates the reality we live in.

Our state of consciousness, our every thought, automatically directs everything we do. Thought is always connected with materialization because thought is merely a subtle frequency of a crude phenomenon. Crude matter and thought, idea, are one and the same thing, but in different dimensions. Thought is the finest, and physical form the crudest expression of the same thing and reality. Thought is information for shaping every phenomena and matter. It should be clear to us why we always attract the events that happen to us, every reality. We are not aware of it, so it seems that some outer force and reality of the outside world has imposed it on us.

For both the positive and the negative, the same rule applies. We always attract what we are in tune with. It happens automatically. It is not necessary for us to deliberately try to attract some favorable reality, because it is already here, we should merely permit the manifestation of it. We will allow this when we cease to hold on to all the negative states and undesirable realities. The hardest obstacle is releasing the negative states and realities, because they are based on the illusion of substantiality and objective materiality; therefore, they are in the reverse direction from the real state of affairs - that everything is current and unsubstantial, that the foundation of everything is consciousness and energy, and that the entirety of existence is based on a divine consciousness which is no different from ourselves. It is also logical that all the negativity is based on the opposition of the divine reality, which is positive.

The illusion that the world is material and objective, separate and away from us, and different from our essence, is the basis for all negative feelings and states, and consequently all negative realities. It is enough for us to, just for a fraction of a second, understand this concept and be inspired to alter every negative state we live in to a positive one.

To summarize the above, it is not necessary for us to attract good states, nor to repel the negative, but only to allow the good ones to express themselves. We attract them anyhow with the very consciousness of our soul, and the negative ones are released because they are not in accordance with our nature. The release in both cases is the only real problem. It is a problem of identification of the lower mind, energy investment in the lower chakras - but more about that in the chapters to follow.

There is one more thing to know about parallel realities.

The essence of the parallel potential for all possible realities is the momentary nature of the quantum field. The finest energy vibrations emanate from the field until they turn into crude physical reality. However, the crude physical reality in its quantum essence still remains just a momentary vibration; therefore, there are no objects real per se. The objects seem that way only because of the nature of our perception. Every moment of a single vibration of the quantum field is one reality. Since there is no time in the quantum field, all the realities are in parallel.

Parallel realities have a wide range of transitional phases, from the quantum field to the crude physical reality that we are able to perceive. However, there are parallel realities that are invisible to our perception. The difference between some of them is so subtle, one can hardly tell the difference; or we may notice it only later, upon reflection. These can be mood swings or states of consciousness we do not notice until something happens as a result. These are changes in reality within our mind, and it functions in pretty much the same way: all possible states of mind already exist in parallel, and we simply cross over from one to the other. They could also be subtle changes in our environment. Some changes amongst them are faster, and some are slower.

Some changes refer to the assorted dimensions, some to the world of ideas, some to the crude forms, and therefore their actualization is diverse. Some changes of reality refer to one conscious subject, some to two, and some to the multitude of subjects that interact with one another. Their actualization depends on this. Some realities serve as the basis for the realization of the other realities. For example, some space is suitable for accommodating many different realities. The house we live in, the city or the country may be a wide concept of reality where many individual realities take place. Therefore, there are wider and narrower fields of reality, and a system of subordination between them. Planet Earth is probably the widest foundation of reality, and carries many other realities on top of itself. This is why there is coherence in space and time in the crude physical world we live in, for the parallel realities to be able to shift into all their forms, from the finest to the crudest.

During the creation of reality there is a collective effect; people create a certain reality they live in together, to such a degree that it may be hard for an individual to change it on his own. For some realities it takes collective work and effort, and for others individual effort will suffice. It depends on the nature of the reality that is being changed. Realities exist in many dimensions and proportions. For some realities it is enough to try altering our way of thinking; for others a little hard work is necessary; for some we have to try for years; and still yet for others it is necessary for entire nations to spill rivers of blood, sweat and tears to affect a change. All of these realities are intermingled, from our morning mood to the centuries old development of human civilizations.

In the creation of a personal reality, the topic of our research in the current life and our karmic experiences have significant leverage. We all have the given subject and life program in accordance with our karmic maturity. We came into this world, which means that we cannot choose our realities in which we live and experience life infinitely. The topic for each life was decided before birth, and generally dominates each life experience, but not unconditionally - only to the point of being brought to a state of awareness. Then experiences can change and continue on a higher level. Consciousness and correct understanding always change reality. One same life reality will keep repeating itself and we remain locked within it, because we are unaware of what is happening to us, because we refuse to accept responsibility for it, because we refuse to acknowledge that it's there for the purpose of personal growth and increased awareness, because we blame other people for our experiences. In the holographic universe there are no "others". We are the conscious subject of everything that is happening.

Finally, parallel realities would not be what they are if there were no options for a complete transition from one reality to another, with no continuity. Still, for the conscious subject a transition of this kind is quite rare and actually needless, because every conscious subject in this world requires continuity of reality to live, and all changes need to be continuous to maintain awareness of their nature and a sense of what is happening. If a conscious subject leaps from one reality into another, he/she would be unable to complete the task for which he/she exists. A partial crossing between very different realities happens to us during sleep, when in deep sleep with no dreams. A complete crossing from one reality into another always happens spontaneously to all of us after the death of the physical body. Such a natural crossing to a completely different reality is the only one that is justified. Anything other than this would be an abuse of position and a conflict of interest for the conscious subject throughout their process of growing in awareness of existence and consciousness itself.

THE DIMENSIONS OF EXISTENCE

Across all esoteric traditions, the nature of reality is described using the four elements: earth, water, fire, and air. These elements symbolically represent the dimensions of reality. The most thorough description is in the Jewish Kabalah, where these elements were detailed impeccably in the teaching of the tetragrammaton. The Tetragrammaton is a four-letter word - JHVH - consisting of the Hebrew letters Yod, Heh, Vav, and Heh. The "name of god," Jehovah, comes from this and was used by commoners who were not aware of the fact (they were not initiated in esoteric knowledge) that this formula, JHVH, represents the four-pole principle of the universal creation of the world through the four elements. At the same time, it represents all of the dimensions of existence, the four dimensions of reality in accordance to which everything in nature manifests and materializes, ranging from information to crude material shapes.

In the Bible it is said that God created humans in his image, which suggests that the human is a microcosm, and that all cosmic laws and principles are compressed into the human, as a cosmos in miniature. This actually points to the holographic model of existence, where every tiny part contains the pattern of the whole; nature knows no divisions.

There is one more element or principle on top of those mentioned above, known as "ether", which in Eastern traditions is called "*akasha*", meaning space, as discussed above. Ether enables all of the other elements, in the same way that space enables everything else in existence. Therefore, the primary cause of the existence of everything, of all forms of existence, is space (Ether or *akasha*). Therefore, we have the following order in the dimensions of reality:

Ether
Air
Fire
Water
Earth

Air, fire, water and earth symbolically represent the universal principles of the processes of manifestation of everything. Ether or *akasha* is immaterial and irreducible, a key principle in the manifestation and the extensiveness of these other elements. Likewise, ether corresponds to the quantum field in physics.

Since the human is a microcosm, different dimensions of man's being can be divided according to the elements in the following way:

The pure presence of consciousness and awareness belongs to the element ether (*akasha*).

The element of air, which symbolizes the "inspiration" of ideas, is the consciousness which is shaped and keeps shaping those ideas, through thoughts and mental patterns. This is the first way in which consciousness is actualized.

The element of fire is the area of mental activity, the exchange of ideas, the preparation and input of energy into their realization, expressing one's will in accordance with mental patterns. The element of fire is created when air and ether combine, or when the pure consciousness is actualized as an idea or a thought. Together they cannot be expressed any differently than as the force that powers creation, in the form of energy.

When ether, air and fire combine - in other words, pure consciousness, idea and driving force - the element of water is created. This symbolizes how, in the (astral) imagination, one suitable idea is selected from the multitude of options, and with emotional identification it is kept in one steady, concrete and visible shape, where the energy is focused, which is finally realized as a physical experience.

For example: car manufacturing is present in the element of air only as pure fiction, as an idea regarding faster mobility; on the level of fire all of the possible models of vehicles ever constructed are present; and on the plane of water one specific and carefully designed shape (model) is chosen, and consequently with the constant energy input coming from those higher dimensions it is realized on the earthly plane by means of physical work. Everything that exists in the physical world follows this process, and getting better acquainted with this allows humans to achieve a higher level of creativity. Everything we create using our imagination and ideas (air and fire) and experience with our emotions in the astral (water) materializes on planet earth.

It is of crucial importance that we comprehend one fact concerning ether, which corresponds to the quantum field: it is at the foundation of everything, or beyond everything, much like the space that enables everything. The microcosm is simultaneously at our essential consciousness with which we are always present in all dimensions and in our Being; it is simultaneously our essential consciousness with which we are always present in all dimensions and with which we can be aware of all dimensions. Furthermore, the microcosm is the entire process of materialization with which we can be aware of all dimensions, and the entire process of materialization. If consciousness were not above it, we would not be able to become aware of it.

It is also important to understand that in the ether or the quantum field, everything is already in its potential state, while the creation of everything in the lower dimensions is merely the actualization of these potentials. Everything is simply in its warped (hidden, implicit) or its developed (manifested, explicit) state of one and the same thing. Everything is so because there is only one divine particle, and there exists only a single divine consciousness which acts in this manner. There is no multitude.

As a result of all of this, it is imperative that we comprehend that the power of creation lies within the power to act, which comes from the finest levels - the levels of pure consciousness of the quantum field or ether. The more we act from the source of consciousness while understanding the process in the other dimensions, the more efficient we become.

HUMANS ARE A MICROCOSM COMPRISED OF ALL THE DIMENSIONS OF NATURE

Dimensions of the divine consciousness in nature are the energy centers, better known as chakras, in man.

The universe exists according to the holographic principle: everything is reflected in everything. The holographic principle of the universe is not chaotic, but follows the anthropic principle, according to which the fundamental constants of nature function the way they do in order to enable the conscious subject into existence - more accurately the awareness of itself in existence, which together with the divine consciousness expresses itself the most distinctly in man. For this reason, the microcosm (man's being) is comprised of all the dimensions of nature.

It was said that we as human beings were created "in the image of God", meaning as the microcosm, because we are comprised of all the dimensions of nature: from ether or the pure consciousness of itself; from the element of air or the mental body and thoughts; from the element of fire which provides us intent and will power; from the element of water which provides us emotions and imagination; and from the element of earth for our physical body.

This is why we can physically exist (earth), feel (water), have willpower (fire) and think (air). Dimensions of all of nature, comprised in our being as the microcosm, make all of this possible for us.

The pure consciousness of itself is from the *akasha* or ether, which is the universal quantum field, and by means of progressive multiplication of the potential of the consciousness of itself, using the mind or the mental body, the body of will and the emotional body shape the physical body. This is why we are able to have a physical body, feelings, will and mind. That is the way the soul's consciousness chose to manifest itself in this world, through us. That, at the same time, is the way we have come to forget the consciousness of our soul.

Human being is the tetragrammaton.

Through human being, the universe creates itself and brings itself into a state of awareness in all of its dimensions.

All other beings exist in a limited way; they do not have all of the dimensions within themselves, they are restricted to only one dimension and a specific manner of perception.

On the level of the element of air, all of the potentials for existence that have been timelessly compressed in ether or the quantum field are expressed as pure ideas, possibilities; they are expressed in us in the form of thoughts. All of the objects are there as ideas. All of the thoughts exist already, as do all of the other realities. No thought is ever new or uniquely ours. It simply takes place in us, but because of the closeness of the consciousness of our soul, the world of ideas changes very quickly in our heads, and tests all of its potentials.

We can merely combine the already existing thoughts and repeat some of them so that, at one point, they begin to seem like our own. We never think, and we are never the creators of our thoughts. Thoughts exist in the form of a world of ideas of the existence itself. This world of ideas in us tests, in its most apparent form, all of its possibilities, due to the proximity of the consciousness of our soul that resides in our human body. The soul's consciousness is the prime attractor of the events of nature, leading to its spiritual goal, as the meaning of all that is happening, and as the divine consciousness of the Absolute. For this reason, this final sense can only be realized in humans themselves and through humans themselves.

Although thoughts are never uniquely ours, and they are all already in existence, we can restructure them in a new way, in a way which perfects the meaning of actions. That is our task in this world. Thought already exists - like bricks we use to build different houses, palaces or prisons. *If we only used the thoughts we fall under the causality of nature and we are conditioned by it. To the degree we are capable of creating new ideas and perfecting our reality, we are able to overcome the conditionality of nature.* This makes all the difference between slavery and freedom. We can have new ideas only with a better connection to the soul's consciousness while still residing in the human body. That is the only way for us to be more aware of reality, and we can find means to implement this consciousness here.

In the element of fire, ideas get shaped into the form of energy, and they are recognized as energy. It is expressed in us like an intention or will to make a certain idea come true, so as not to remain sheer fiction. All of the objects exist in the form of energy, intention or the will to realize this idea in the element of fire.

In the element of water, the idea is united with intention and will, and receives concrete shapes in the world of imagination, along the astral plane, which corresponds with our emotional body. All objects exist here in their astral form, where we can concretely use our fancy and visualize them, with every detail.

When all of these preceding elements join together, an object that previously existed as an idea only, where the energy was invested in and transformed into an astral shape, it materializes in the element of earth as a concrete physical shape, a thing or an event. Then we can take it in our hands and touch it.

All of these elements exist and act together. When we are aware of something, when we see an object, a thought is formed in our mind which automatically identifies it. We name it using our thoughts, we identify everything we see. Later we do not repeat it, but it goes without saying in our system that we know what it is. We do this with every object we see for the first time: we identify it with our thoughts, we think it through, we give it a name. We all do this all the time, we always identify and explain everything, what it is and how it should be done - from an infant innocently pointing in the direction of an object, to the scientist on the verge of discovering some cosmological truth.

All of the phenomena and all of the objects already exist simultaneously in the world of ideas, as well as on the physical plane. For example, we hold a rock in our hands, and in our mind we know it is a rock. These are parallel realities of one and the same phenomenon. This same object, the "thought-rock", exists separately, because the nature of reality splits it into multiple dimensions. It is layered and expressed through those dimensions. In the element of air some object exists as a thought we have in us about the object in question, while at the same time we have this object in our hand as the physically materialized item. That is one and the same phenomenon, where only the difference in dimension diverts them from an outer object to an inner thought. The thought is within, the object is without.

The thought in us is just as real as the objects in the outside world. Only the varying dimensions separate them so that they seem to differ.

To realize our ideas all we have to do is bring to awareness and harmonize all of the processes that we go through, from an idea to materialization.

For this reason, the human is tetragrammaton, who embodies all the dimensions of nature. Only humans have the consciousness that this entire process of creation and materialization of everything into one harmonious whole. At the same time, and for the same reason, only humans experience the illusion of thinking that they are separate processes.

The divine consciousness of the Absolute enables everything in different dimensions, from the highest and the finest, ether, down to the three-dimensional physical world represented by the element of earth. It is a process that grows cruder and cruder with every step, where the world of ideas keeps being transformed into a concrete shape. This is a simultaneous process happening instantly: what is a thought in the world of ideas or the element of air, is at the same time a concrete shape of some being or phenomena in the physical world on earth. It is one and the same, but due to the nature of multidimensionality of existence there is a difference in perception - and this is the only real difference, seemingly it looks like some process is happening over the course of time and via a series of separate occasions. Our nervous system and sensory perception were designed to slow down the current events of entire existence to the degree where it would seem to be a gradual process happening over a period of time.

Every form of motion is in reality one and the same motion, from the changing thoughts to the movement of the body, but due to the various dimensions it appears as an alternate movement, a separate phenomenon, even seemingly unrelated. The one responsible for this separating but also uniting is the human mind (*manas*). The same way in which a crystal prism refracts light into all the colors of the rainbow, the exact same way, dimensions (which a human being comprises) separate the Unity into a multitude of phenomena and forms.

The illusion of creation of the world as the multitude is just a consequence of an individual consciousness moving through the various dimensions. In fact, it is all just one acting within one, within itself, in the divine absolute as its imagination. In the perfect knowing of the divine absolute, nothing moves; everything is just itself – every shape and every movement is merely the confirmation and affirmation of itself. This recursive affirmation of everything is consciousness.

THE NATURE OF CONSCIOUSNESS

We have analyzed the nature of consciousness while speaking on the nature of existence. Perhaps all that remains is for us to stress the essence of the nature of consciousness.

Consciousness is the outcome of existence. Consciousness is simply existence that has manifested or actualized all of its possibilities, its fullest potential, to itself - although it is not unknown to itself. Consciousness is existence that has reached its purpose, meaning or outcome, its realization.

Existence happens completely outside of the notion of time; time does not exist because existence, on its finest quantum level, *akasha*, already exists in its entirety. That is why awareness of existence may appear at any time, it can go back to itself, while it is still in existence during the process of awareness. **The ultimate goal of existence, consciousness, may reach every act of existence. It does so, frequently, and at any given moment.** This is why we have awareness of existence. It is possible because it surpasses the process of time. Consciousness in us is evidence that time does not exist in the essence of existence. When consciousness exists in us, it is partially limited by the illusion of time, but it always keeps its full potential, otherwise it would not be consciousness. That is why consciousness is always linked to something good, nice or perfect.

Consciousness is existence itself, which is becoming aware of itself. This becoming aware of itself always happens through man. In all other shapes, existence merely exists in a potential form. Only through humans is existence able to reach awareness of itself, because humans are the only beings capable of transcending time and realizing the purpose of existence; they have this capability because they have a soul which, in the long run, is the very outcome of existence.

Consequently, existence without consciousness is not possible, and neither is consciousness without existence.

The very fact that consciousness exists proves that existence is timeless, that the outcome of any existence already exists in its most subtle form in the quantum level. Since the quantum field already possesses the potential of all possible events in time and space, of all of existence, consciousness exists and is able to be the foundation of all of existence. This foundation can be referred to as the quantum field or as the quantum consciousness.

The essence of consciousness is in the surpassing of any possible form of existence and its objective cognition. Therefore, consciousness is transcendental in its essence. 'Transcendental' means that what surpasses, what is beyond. Consciousness is always above every form of existence because we are able to become aware of every form of existence, of every phenomenon. If the consciousness were not able to do this, we would not be aware of existence itself. Therefore, we can safely say that consciousness is the outcome or the aspiration of existence - its attempt to get to know itself, its every shape and all of its possibilities.

All life forms aspire to reach consciousness. Plants have consciousness, as do animals, and humans most of all. All life forms have been rewarded with some degree of awareness of existence and this awareness does not differ greatly from their existence. It is determined by their existence; in other words, they are aware of the object only. Only humans can have both awareness of existence, and awareness of themselves in that existence - the awareness of the object and the subject alike. Only humans can discover a sense of the overall existence; first by becoming aware of themselves. This is because human essence is no different from the consciousness that enables that very existence. Human essence is transcendental, the human soul is not of this world, although the world in its entirety exists as the projection of the soul's consciousness, as per its intelligent design.

THE SOUL'S CONSCIOUSNESS
AND ITS INCARNATION INTO THE BODY
THROUGH THE HIGHER MIND

The divine Absolute, as everything-that-is, expresses itself as everything-that-can-be by implementing the process of individuation. The first individuation of awareness of the Absolute itself is the monad of consciousness, known to us as the soul. Souls are monads of the consciousness of the divine Absolute, its individual emanation or manifestation.

These monads of the divine consciousness, or souls, create all potential life forms in order to be able to express all of the potentials of the divine Absolute. They create the cosmos and all of the life in it.

Every soul individualizes itself further, so as to experience all of the possibilities of life in a finer and more accurate way. The final or finishing individuation of the awareness of the soul takes place in the shape of humans - their being and life.

The principle is as follows: the divine Absolute cannot exist without manifesting itself, otherwise it would be abstract or nothing. It has to manifest as the overall existence, in the form of all of the possibilities of existence. Every possible form of existence, every phenomenon, event or object is manifested by the Absolute itself. Getting to know every option is then awareness of this existence. The divine Absolute projects itself into a multitude of individual monads of consciousness that are meant to gather as many impressions of all the life as possible, to retrieve them for the divine Absolute as the awareness of itself. It appears as if it is circulating; in reality the only thing that is timelessly happening is the

Absolute itself, for nothing is possible outside of it. Everything else is circulation within its sphere, simultaneously and in parallel. Existence is like a mirror which reflects the image of the divine Absolute, and the Absolute getting to know itself in existence is pure consciousness.

This understanding itself is timeless, which means that it has already taken place, and keeps taking place at any given moment. That is why consciousness is the very essence of existence itself, independent of any life form. It is not a process bound in time; time is a collective illusion of our individual perception. However, we do not see that from the perspective of the divine Absolute, but from our individual and very restricted perspective which progresses with linear time. Linear time is needed in our perception to facilitate the chronological course of actions, together with all of their details, in the perception of man. This detail would not be possible if there were no linear time and no three-dimensional space.

Therefore, monads of the consciousness of the divine Absolute become individual souls which begin to gather varied impressions while going through the drama of life, and the consciousness of these impressions is delivered to the divine Absolute as awareness of existence, as its awareness of itself. At the end of the reincarnation cycle, once they have learnt the meaning of existence, souls return to their source, to what they actually are - to the divine Absolute - although this is what they have still been during the course of their illusory existence, for nothing at all is possible outside of the divine Absolute. Everything is merely itself. In the soul of man, this knowing is manifested in its strongest and purest way as the state of samadhi.

The same divine consciousness manifests in the form of elements and minerals, and on this level experiences all of the possibilities of matter and the combination of elements. Afterwards, it manifests through plant life where (apart from an even more complex shaping), it becomes acquainted with the most rudimentary form of perception and experiences the first, simplest movements. Then the divine consciousness is manifested in animal form where, with enhanced methods of shaping, it perfects the power of movement and sensory perception. All plant and animal life forms are nothing but a scaffolding upon which movement and perception is perfected. Animal life forms maximally perfect movement and sensory perception through the food chain.

All animals are food for one another; some are hunters and predators, and some are prey; some have to develop the ability to move and perceive for foraging; and others as a self-preservation mechanism. In this practical way the power to move and perceive the divine consciousness is developed in animals. Finally, the human shape evolves and possesses all of the sensory and action organs, as well as one more thing that animals lack – the individual mind which enables humans to utilize tools and not just their body. Humans have speech and uses spoken words which enables the memorization and safekeeping of information; their exchange allows for a far quicker propensity for collecting impressions from all of the potentials of existence than all plant and animal life combined.

Unlike the lower forms of existence, which are limited to survival only, humans experience the drama of life – the events and the odyssey of all of their options that exceed sheer survival. Humans have karma with which they collect impressions of existence in the space of many incarnations and through assorted deeds. Through the karmic drama and the power to act, humans appreciate the meaning of all that is happening, the good and the evil, the real and illusory, and through this realization they crystallize the quality of consciousness of existence, thus returning themselves to their source, the divine Absolute.

Unlike minerals, plants and animals that have developed perception of all the possible life forms, humans are in possession of the mind with which they are able to perceive; they can visualize things independently of time and space, and they also have the perception of meaning of phenomena, find meaning in their work and deeds. This is the most subtle part of awareness of existence. Karma means work, acts and deeds, as well as the consequences of actions. Therefore, karma means awareness of causes and consequences of our actions and events. But the perception of the awareness of existing is not enough, actions must also be performed, and consequently, humans must ascertain what the outcome of their actions are. Humans become aware of their actions and the consequences of their actions, and in this way the meaning of every possible action and event returns to the divine source, as awareness of itself. The final cognition of the meaning of all of the possible events in existence, the phenomenon itself, equals the ultimate consciousness of the divine Absolute itself.

Therefore, it can be said that the meaning of existence is in perception and its refinement.

The soul is not incarnated into a body in its entirety; only a tiny fragment is. The soul's consciousness branches out like a tree into ever smaller limbs. Its strength is too great for it to fit in its entirety in any body. And that is not necessary. In the body we can find merely the potential for soul's consciousness, which is enough for the life of that body and for collecting impressions of existence. Gathering impressions of all the potentialities of existence reifies the presence of the soul in the body. However, this process must come from the body itself, where awareness happens for the very first time, when it is separate and estranged from the whole (to which it originally belongs). This tiny and seemingly estranged consciousness in the body is the human ego, the little "I" or the physical mind. It is the everyday consciousness of the mind that a normal human uses while being in an awakened state in this world.

This little mind/ego, identified with the physical body, is the ultimate point of projection of the divine consciousness of itself, into something else, into its opposition. The eclipse of awareness of itself happens here. Such a human is completely alienated from a source; void of a sense of belonging in this world. But nothing is possible outside of the whole of the divine Absolute and therefore, such a human condition is nothing but an illusion. This illusion of separation from one's self is at the same time the ultimate point of creativity of the divine consciousness. To have an individual consciousness which is convinced that it is separate from everything, is the ultimate point of creativity of everything that Is. It is the final stage of alienation from oneself needed for the divine consciousness to experience all that is opposite. From this point onwards, the only thing that can happen is a return to the original divine consciousness, and that is the typical, perpetual circumstance of man: they learn everything that can be learnt about the nature of reality and how to live in it. Humans build their lives and develop civilization solely because they have experienced the most opposing point of themselves, of their divine essence. Every human civilization, and all human aspirations, are based on the attempt by humans to return to their divine essence.

This tiny awareness or "I" in the body cannot do much of its own accord. It must receive help from a higher consciousness, from a connection to the soul. The link between the physical mind and the soul's consciousness is the higher "I" or the higher mind. It is not incarnated in the body of man, but it has a perpetual connection with it. The higher mind remains in a higher dimension, between the elements of air and ether, and acts as a go-between, connecting the physical mind with an objective awareness of the soul.

Owing to this connection, the mind can have an objective awareness of itself and every phenomenon. If it were not for this it would have only a physical awareness, much like the animals. The body has an intelligence of its own, very simple and conditioned, but sufficient for survival. The link to the higher mind and the soul's consciousness gives our body everything that makes us human and soulful. This connection can, however, be so feeble in certain individuals that they barely differ from animals; their conduct is heartless and improper. The weaker the link between the mind and the soul's consciousness, the less that person sees the whole picture and of the divine presence in every aspect of life, and the more they feel alienated in all aspects of his life; therefore, negativity prevails in him, and for this reason they are in conflict with reality. He does not possess objective awareness.

The stronger the connection between the physical mind and the higher mind, and the more objective awareness resides in him, the more an individual is aware of their unity with the divine Absolute; their very existence is an expression of the divine consciousness to them, and they are always positive and good because they are able to detect this consciousness as both their own, and of all life as well. Namely, in consciousness there can be no divisions. There is only one consciousness in everything, from the divine Absolute to the tiniest blade of grass or particle, and this same consciousness is in us.

The higher mind has a higher and a wider perspective; it sees from a higher dimension every event in a much wider context, which gives it the ability to pass on this information to the lower, physical mind or ego which has a very limited perspective and is only able to perceive information with its senses, and is within reach. This information, sent to the physical mind, arrives in the form of inspiration or intuition, a sudden insight, in an awakened state or during sleep, when the physical mind is suppressed and the higher mind can hold greater sway.

The physical mind is tied to the body and sensory perception. For this reason, when consciousness leaves the body, humans begin to have much wider and far-reaching perception because they are in contact with higher dimensions and the higher mind. It is enough for the brain and the nervous system, whose job is to slow down and limit awareness, to falter a little or cease to operate (due to some trauma or the drug induced state) for the consciousness of the mind to leave its limitations and start perceiving some of the higher dimensions, some astral phenomenon, or for humans to find themselves in the astral plane of their own will and thereby experience an out-of-body state.

Out-of-body and astral experiences are the best example of connection to the higher mind, because the higher mind does not reside in the body. When consciousness is not limited by the influence of the body, it finds it easier to make a connection to the higher mind.

People who have out-of-body or astral experiences easily have a stronger attachment to the higher mind. A problem may arise due to the fact that the astral plane is very near the physical world and therefore impressions from the physical world remain and begin to mix with the inspiration from the higher mind, so that the bond on the astral plane is not always perfect and pure. But with experience one can purify themselves better.

This is the basic structure of consciousness in man: the **soul's consciousness**, which only partially embodies itself, and the **consciousness of the physical mind**, which connects with the soul's consciousness through the **higher mind**, which is between the physical body and the divine soul's consciousness.

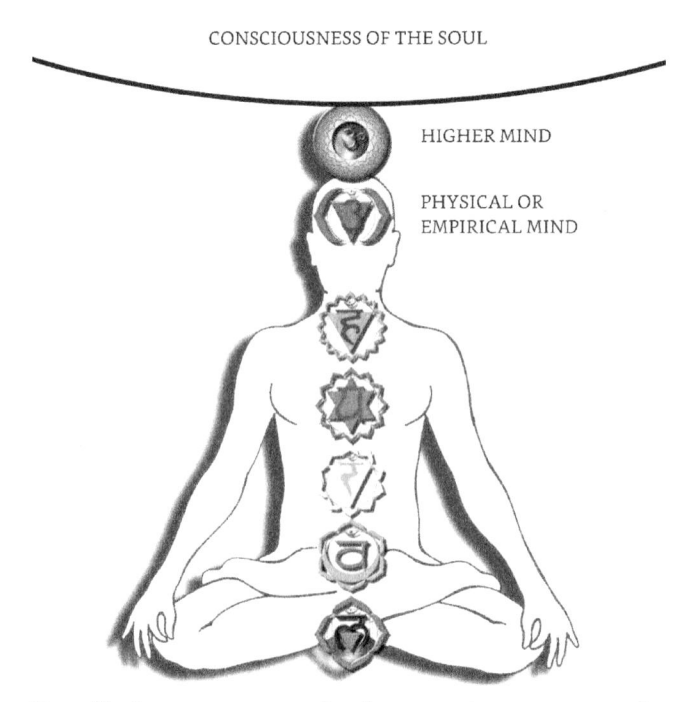

CONSCIOUSNESS OF THE SOUL

HIGHER MIND

PHYSICAL OR EMPIRICAL MIND

All religious or mystical experiences are the reflection of connecting the physical or empirical mind with soul's consciousness using the higher mind.

All of human growth in attaining consciousness and cognition, all unity of consciousness and existence, is due to the increase in the presence of consciousness in the body. Although it can never fully embody itself it can increase its presence in the physical body to the point of turning the body into light.[8] Its presence in the body is generally more visible as goodness, kindness, love, mercy and enlightenment.[9]

The process of presence, growth and decline of awareness in the body is depicted by the chakra system. **Chakras are psychoenergetic junctures of consciousness and existence in the being of man.** Their diversity reflects the versatility of states of consciousness in humans and their method of existence.

The divine consciousness has shaped the entire cosmos through its individual monads or souls, for all of existence. In the memories of souls before birth,[10] found through hypnotic regression, we discover that our souls

---

[8] On the experiences of the manifestation of the soul's consciousness as light, see the work of Mircea Eliade: *"Mephistopheles and the Androgyne"*.

[9] Nikola Tesla expressed the same concept: "Aristotle taught that there was an immovable 'entelechy' in the universe that moves everything and thought was its main attribute. I am also convinced that the whole universe is unified in both the material and spiritual sense. Out there in the universe there is a nucleus that gives us all the power, all the inspiration; it draws us to itself eternally, I feel its mightiness and values it transmits throughout the universe; thus keeping it in harmony. I have not breached the secret of that core, still I am aware of its existence, and when wanting to give it any material attribute I imagine LIGHT, and when trying to conceive its spirituality I imagine BEAUTY and COMPASSION. The one who carries that belief inside feels strong, finds joy in his work, for he experiences himself as a single tone in the universal harmony".

[10] Michael Newton: *"Journey of Souls, Case Studies of Life Between Lives"* (1994).

created all other life forms, all plant and animal species, before they incarnated themselves into our body. At this stage, they were practicing creativity. They were doing so with the aid of the divine consciousness that enables everything, for they originated from the same source. Likewise, from hypnotic regressions, we have true accounts that our soul is projecting our current life and the body we live in. It is only part of the truth.

Actually, we as souls participated in the creation of the universe, the planet earth, all of nature, and all the conditions this body lives in. It is pointless to believe that we created this body but not all of the conditions for this body, as it lives in a holographic universe in which absolutely nothing is divided from the entirety of nature. The earth we tread on, the water we drink, the air we breathe, we have created ourselves – of course not us as this little lost ego of ours, mind identified with body, but we as souls, we as integrated parts of the divine consciousness that enables everything.

Monads of the divine consciousness, the sources of our soul, primarily created cosmic space, followed by the creation of the stars and all the celestial bodies, and all of the conditions necessary for organic life. All of existence is a result of intelligent design - the design of the intelligence of our soul.

UNITY OF CONSCIOUSNESS AND EXISTENCE, OF BODY AND SOUL

When we speak of the unity of consciousness and existence, it all refers to the unity of body and soul.

On a cosmic scale consciousness and existence create the whole universe, and on an individual level the body and soul create the cosmos of events for one individual being, man, and the magic of versatile phenomena otherwise known as karma.

Karma and the nature of events should be understood in the following way.

Boundaries do not exist in nature, in reality; nothing is purely outward, the same way nothing is purely inward. Therefore, the boundaries of our body, our skin, pose no true boundaries to anything. It is only an illusion of the physical (empirical) mind/ego.

All shapes and phenomena in the cosmos are in their essence electromagnetic phenomena. Such is the nature of the quantum field. Above it, on a much rougher plane, existence keeps shaping itself into atomic and molecular form by means of chemical processes, in accordance with the laws of physics. However, at the base of everything is electromagnetism. The cosmos is basically an electromagnetic phenomenon. The stars are a huge electromagnetic phenomenon, and gravity is electrostatic phenomenon on a large scale. Planets are big electromagnets which by their sheer motion (magnetic induction) generate life energy, as well as all events – because there are no boundaries. Life energy and events are one and the same occurrence, taking place on different proportions.

The earth, together with the ionosphere, is one big induction machine, as are all celestial bodies which rotate. (Earth is zero, and ionosphere is phase, and every meter farther from the ground the voltage increases by 100V; with their induction we get thunder and lightning, roughly about a hundred of them each second).

In what way does space constitute our body and character, and events throughout all our life? It does so by moving the largest objects that compose space – by moving the planets and the stars, because a larger whole composes a smaller one. All of it is composed of life energy, and life energy on earth is generated from magnetic induction which originates from the moon and other celestial bodies orbiting around the earth, as well as the earth orbiting the sun. All of these have their origin in the overall electromagnetic background, ether or *akasha*. Planets are magnetic bodies and with their motion they generate life force and all movement of living beings. Consequently, they generate all phenomena, because there are no boundaries in nature. Rules according to which planets bring about events reveals to us the science of astrology.

However, a problem arises in our ability to conceive facts. We admit to the fact that our metabolism, and what happens under our skin, is spontaneous and conditioned by nature, but the same spontaneous and natural conditionality we attribute to macrocosmic phenomena. And everything which is set between the micro and the macrocosm, all our human endeavors, we give a special status, and attribute some "freedom" to it. This is nothing but an illusion of the ego, the physical or empirical mind.

The rotation of the earth moves our body. If the earth and everything in the cosmos stopped, our body would also stop and disintegrate into dust. Without the motion taking place in the cosmos, we would be unable to move. Therefore, unawakened individuals never move of their own accord; they are entirely made up and moved by a larger whole. Based on the same principle that causes the earth to move around the sun, the wind and the clouds, all the living beings on earth move.

The science which demonstrates this wider concept - the planets generating all phenomena, from our body and mind, to character and temperament, to all other manifestations - is the science of astrology. Astrology is a completely empirical science based on the principles that have only recently been discovered and is called "the holographic model of the universe", "the strong anthropic principle" and the "electric cosmos".

We have never breathed air, or produced a single heart beat, much like we never did anything else in our life; it was all performed by nature while we were imagining "I did it" or "that is my being". Any notion of our individuality and independent action is sheer fantasy. It is all One. Nothing is our own. Everything belongs to the whole. Following this simple principle, every being in the universe can recognize the entire universe.

Our awareness of this unity of nature also means that our essence surpasses it. We are the transcendental soul, and not nature. Due to this fact, we can be aware of everything in nature. This lid of natural conditionality is not entirely shut. In all this conditionality, the consciousness of the transcendental soul has found a way to sneak in. This is the beginning of the story of man, of karma. Soul's consciousness brings forth the principle of freedom which liberates from karma, and conditionality to the degree it is present in existence, in the body and all actions. Soul's consciousness attracts events to their meaning, to awareness of the self. Nature is self-sufficient - the jungle is full of life - but nothing would exist in this world were it not for the soul's consciousness that found its way to infiltrate itself further and further into the body. Everything that humans make using their skills and hands came about in this way.

The gradual descent of consciousness into the body and its impact through the body is best expressed in the psychoenergetic centers in the body, otherwise known as chakras.

Human deeds are a combination of natural conditionality and conscious freedom. The combination of all planetary influences, which defines the science of astrology, constitutes all the phenomena we are exposed to. However, we are not always passive in this, it is not everything that happens. We have come here as souls to introduce the principle of awareness and meaning, the understanding of everything, and the awareness of this will bring freedom to action. The more awareness and understanding we bring into life and existence, the more we reduce the conditionality of nature.

Nature requests this of us - to make itself fully aware in the tiniest detail - and then it withdraws. This happens in the world and it happens in man, to each and every one of us. All of human karma consists of an effort to consciously overcome the area of the unconscious and conditioned. To a large extent, we are mere witnesses in this world, who only occasionally act in accordance with their own will. To increase the ratio of conscious actions using our own will takes several lives or incarnations. When, in the last life of the incarnation cycle, we master conscious actions and attain free will, we have set ourselves free, and at the same time we have fulfilled the purpose of nature's existence, full understanding, not just as witnesses but through our actions as well.

We are here to give purpose to all existence.

In order to understand the relationship between natural conditionality and will correctly, one should remember the following definition: **humans have free will only in their attempt towards acquiring knowledge and awareness, towards the awakening, the strengthening of the presence of consciousness in the body. If they act driven by any other urges or reasons, they always act out of natural conditionality. The reason for this is that soul's consciousness is the principle of freedom in nature.** Therefore, only if they act out of soul's consciousness can they overcome natural conditionality. Any other deed is completely conditioned by natural causality, although they find it hard to perceive this because conditionality is so overwhelming and complex that humans develop a conviction that it does not exist, that they act out of his own free will and independently, or only occasionally they will admit to incidents of conditionality. The reason for this is that conditionality traps the mind, the mind being the finest informative activity of nature. The unconscious human possesses neither will nor freedom. The will and freedom to act independently can be received only from consciousness of the soul, because his soul is transcendental as regards the mind and nature, independent and always free.

Therefore, when we learn and work on ourselves for the sake of raising awareness, we act against natural conditionality and we overcome it. When humans behave like this, they radiate nobility, dignity and excellence. Such conduct is a source of joy to man; maybe not immediate joy, but most definitely permanent. Human creativity derives from overcoming this conditionality of nature. When we follow natural impulses without directing them toward awareness and learning, our actions are that of a machine, completely conditioned by the wider context, although we keep deceiving ourselves that we act of our own free will, driven by some illusory, subjective reasons. The reason for this is that our mind is just as conditioned as our body. When humans acts like this they are no different from any other conditioned being who is a slave to their natural instincts. Without soul's consciousness man is low and pathetic. These actions are the cause of all of the suffering people experience in this world.

The bottom line is that humans cannot influence the outer world before they change themselves. By changing themselves, they change the outside world in the best possible way. In fact, they can only change themselves, for that is the only freedom they have; in the outer world everything is conditioned by the wider context (by astrological and other rules). Therefore, we can have an impact on the outside world only indirectly, by means of changing ourselves. The results are always visible; the more correctly we raise the level of our awareness, the more favourable our life is. And vice versa: all the pain and suffering of life stems from human unconsciousness.

The principle of relation of consciousness and existence, of the nature and spirit, was stated in antiquity in the text of the classical *sankhya: Sankhya-karika by Ishvarakrshna* (verse 57): Just as insentient milk serves as nourishment for the calf, so too does Nature (prakrti) act for the sake of the Self's emancipation (soul, *purusha*)". Verse 59: "Just as the dancer desists from dancing having shown herself to spectators, so too does primal Nature (prakrti) desist having revealed itself to the Self (soul)". Verse 61: "Nothing, in my view, is gentler and more gracious than Nature; once aware of having been seen, Nature does not expose herself to the gaze of the Self (soul)."

All of this has been known in the Gnostic Gospels and particularly in the Manichaean Studies (Hegemonius, Acta Archelai, 8. Bar Khoni, Scholia, 315, 22-27) that emphasize the astrological influence of incarnation cycles of souls in the body: "When the Omnipotent God saw the way of suffering of the soul in the body he called for the Paraclete. He, having arrived, prepared everything required for the task of saving souls. He constructed the wheel with twelve vessels. Put into motion by the celestial spheres, this wheel captures the dying souls, and the raft is being embarked with the dying souls, and then disembarked... into Aeons, where they remain in the Pier of Glory called the Perfect Man... It is the pier of light, because it is filled with purified souls."

Therefore, if there is conditionality, there also is the unconditionality this conditionality resides on. The freedom of unconditionality is at the heart of all phenomena, although they appear in the outer rougher world as conditioned ones. Even though the world is conditioned, it is in a paradoxical way constructed as the perfect means for expressing unconditionality. In other words, ***irrelevant of how conditioned it is, this world is perfectly set for human enlightenment. There is nothing else and nothing better we can do than to become enlightened.*** In fact, the very insight of conditionality of the world sets us free. The very notion of "setting our soul free" goes hand-in-hand with overcoming the non-freedom, the overcoming which can only be achieved with objective awareness, with a clear insight or realizing what conditionality really is.

All of the conditionality of the world is orchestrated in such a way that all the unconditioned divine consciousness that makes everything possible is able to express itself. It does so through humans. If it were not so, the world would be nothing but a dark dungeon with no life in sight; instead, it is a vast array of creativity and beauty. The beauty of existence and the infinity of the cosmos is proof that no matter what conditionality exists locally, the unconditioned divine consciousness far outweighs it. This divine consciousness is the essence of our soul.

Only two things are infinite and unconditioned: the cosmos and the human soul. Both are, in their essence, one and the same unconditionality. The more that a human is spiritual, the more they are assured of this.

IF EVERYTHING IS A REFLECTION OF DIVINE CONSCIOUSNESS, WHY IS THERE EVIL IN THE WORLD?

The story of the nature of existence and consciousness would not be complete if we did not give an answer to the obvious question: if everything is a reflection of the divine consciousness, why is there evil in the world?

We have stated that the divine Absolute manifests itself in the form of monads of consciousness which further branch out to even finer shapes, known to us as souls. They are our essence. Everything is manifested as an aspiration of the divine Absolute, in order to experience all of its potentials, all of the aspects of its existence - because the divine consciousness cannot live without manifestation of this kind. *The divine consciousness is bound to express itself as every possible form of existence,* and for this reason, the nature of existence expresses all of the possibilities of existence. Souls are the conscious subjects that gather all of the experiences of existence and bring them back to the divine Absolute, as the awareness of itself.

Here we have a paradox. Souls as the emanation of the divine consciousness are pure, good, beautiful and perfect. Therefore, people as the carriers of souls in this world cannot possibly be negative and evil. They, because of their soul, see the divine consciousness in all of existence and recognize it as their own consciousness, as the divine presence.

This quality of their nature causes two problems.

The first is that, because of the strong presence of the soul's consciousness within them and the consciousness of the omnipresent divine consciousness, people seldom have an interest in hard work and the development of culture. They see that everything is already perfect, that existence itself rests on the divine consciousness, and for that reason soulful people are naturally religious, and nothing much interests them, apart from submitting themselves to the divine - not even the development of their material culture and technology. All of the saints and enlightened people testify this; those who have come to the point of realizing the full soul's consciousness in their body.

These people can live in huts and caves. They are even proud to. Their lack of material interest is considered to be proof of their spirituality – but it's merely an indication of an immature and naive spirituality. True spirituality relies on transcendence, on the overcoming of all divisions - the division of material and spiritual included - because matter as such does not exist, and the spiritual can never cease to be, because consciousness is the foundation of all existence. True spirituality is in the creative manifesting of consciousness into existence, in the creativity that sees no boundaries between consciousness and existence, which reveals existence as consciousness and consciousness as existence.

The second problem that souls face is with the task of experiencing all the possible states of being, including the negative ones all of the opposites, even the opposites of everything that is good and nice, the opposite of the divine presence. This is what the material world was created for. Souls cannot experience this of their own accord. They need assistance, the assistance of beings that do not possess the same awareness of the soul and the divine presence and which therefore find it easier to commit evil acts, i.e. the illusion of the opposite to the divine good. Due to their lack of soul, they think there is nothing divine, that the matter they perceive with their senses is everything, and that acting for the sake of survival is perfectly justifiable, even if it hurts others.

For the monads of consciousness or souls to be forced to experience all states of existence, even the most negative, the divine Absolute manifested itself into good souls that are aware of their divine source, and also into entities that have a far greater illusion of the separation from the divine source. These negative entities were named Satanic or Luciferian.

The divine Absolute has manifested itself in the following proportions: **two thirds** of the monads of consciousness bear in themselves the awareness of their divine source (the angel entities); and **one third** of monads whose entities do not possess this awareness to a sufficient degree (Satanic, demonic and Luciferian entities). This proportion was required because, for the positive to win, it takes twice as much power than the negative.

Destructive negative processes are always easier because they are based on the illusion of separation from the divine source and the unity of everything, which is strong in the lower dimensions, and the strongest in physical reality.

Negative entities are everywhere, side by side with the positive. They play the role of tempters that introduce coercion and pressure on soul-bearers, to experience what they themselves cannot: negative states or so-called 'evil'.

In order to understand the nature of negative entities we must understand the history of the human species. According to exoteric science taught in schools, all life was created by accidental collisions of particles, and we human beings were created by accidental DNA division, or rather by a mistake in the division of the DNA, which originated in the apes. Since we have not made much progress from the apes, we tend to be negative.

However, there is an esoteric science and it reveals to us a different, alternative, but much more interesting history. It tells us that the original existence of the first human beings with the divine soul as their essence, in this galaxy, was in the constellation of Lyra. Gradually, over time, they further and further descended down to this material world, in order to acquire experience of all the options of existence; this descent gradually made them lose the connection with their divine source. They came into conflict with the negative entities (whose task was to force Lyrans to experience the numerous possibilities the physical world has to offer as well as opposition to existence) and consequently, as a result of this conflict, the descendants of Lyrans, human beings with soul's consciousness, moved to many constellations: the Pleiades, Tau Ceti, Eridanus, Procyon, Arcturus, and many others.

In the many battles with negative entities that followed, and even in conflict with each other, they realized they were losing their connection to the divine source. All of the knowledge and technology they possessed was thanks to their remembrance of the divine source; but the memory was fading fast.

For this reason, they were forced to make one desperate move in the evolution of the divine consciousness, a move that represents a turning point back to the divine source. This final move, occurring at the furthest point in the oblivion of the divine, after which only a return to the divine source is possible, resulted in the creation of humans on planet Earth, in their image. They combined all of the chief characteristics of their genetics to create humans on earth.

To make human development maximally dynamic, for the purpose of acquiring all possible experiences, three things were done.

Firstly, the human life span was reduced tenfold in order to speed up human development - from 800 years to 80.

Secondly, together with the Earth, the whole solar system was made, as an external factor in human psychodynamics and organic life on Earth in general. On the influence of psychodynamics on humans we have developed the science of astrology. Science will start to convey discoveries on the key role the planets of the solar system play on all organic life on Earth in the centuries to come.

Gnostics knew some of this; they called the beings who created the solar system the 'Archons', or principalities, the rulers. They considered these beings to be negative because they imprisoned the human soul in the body, and viewed the world as a sort of prison one must escape from. They did not, however, know that the solar system and the Earth were created by our own souls, from a much higher level than the one we are currently on, probably with the aid of advanced beings. For such an undertaking, a qualified workforce was required. It was impossible to perform something like this with a magic wand.

Thirdly, the human body was installed with a system of psychoenergetic centers, otherwise known as chakras, that correlate with the functioning of the solar system. These psychoenergetic centers represent all the states of consciousness in humans, and the connection between the state of consciousness and existence. **By means of chakras, the consciousness is connected to existence through humans. In this way, owing to the chakra system, humans cannot sublimate his consciousness** *without altering his actions, and in accordance with this sublimating, they cannot separate the consciousness from his actions. If they try to do so, they stunt their growth.*

The purpose of the creation of humans on Earth was for the orchestration of the key and "historical" reversal of the divine consciousness, in order for it to return to itself, to its full knowing. This must be done by creating the complete illusion of the oblivion of itself. This illusion of the fullest eclipse of consciousness and existence takes place in the mind and the ego of modern-day humans, who think that the world is nothing but material in the way they are able to perceive so using his senses. This is the rock bottom of the divine consciousness. It is the farthest point of alienation between consciousness and existence. But, if we can envisage this process as a form of circulation, which in fact it is, from this most distant point onwards, the only option is a return to the divine consciousness.

If the divine consciousness constantly returned to itself, based on the constant memory of itself, it would achieve nothing. An illusion of complete separation of oneself and complete oblivion is required in order for it to become fully aware of itself. This separation takes place through human individuality, in the mind and the ego. In fact, only through the completion of the process of individuation of the divine consciousness were the first monads of the Absolute created. The further the process went, ever bigger individuation of consciousness developed. The final individuation is the individuation of ego, which is being closed off into one being and one body with the illusion of complete separation of the being from the whole and from the divine.

This was the starting point of human growth on this planet, and it was the real start of man. Most of the traces of previous civilizations on planet Earth were wiped out, and the development of man began from scratch. Humans were made to learn everything from the beginning, to learn the laws of nature and to develop science and technology on his own, to create their own civilization, not just to inherit it from others, as was previously the case with old human civilizations in other constellations. Because of this, the esoteric knowledge, magic, the knowing of higher dimensions, and the ancient knowledge of old civilizations were forbidden.

In order for development to constantly improve, so that people with human soul would work on creating a civilization by means of perfecting their material environment, science and technology, and to turn their nature towards the spirit and the divine consciousness as the only true continuation of act of creation through man, three key events were designed which triggered, maintained and hastened this flow.

The first event is known in history as the resurrection of Christ. Jesus was a descendant of the old civilization ("the son of man") that used to exist in the area of Mesopotamia; he was a great master of old school esoteric teaching, and he conveyed true knowledge of unifying the consciousness and existence through labor in this world. He also warned people of the existence of non-human beings, and the importance of awareness of the soul. We now measure time from the day he was born. Before him, the old civilizations were measuring everything with natural lunar cycles, which were circular; there was no civilizational development. Since the birth of Christ linear historical time was introduced, which is necessary for the development of science, technology and civilization in general. Hence, Christ is associated with solar symbolism. Chinese and Indian civilizations had huge potential for growth, but they remained the same for thousands of years because they did not have the impulse of expansion that Christianity brought forth.

The second key event required for the development of modern civilization was the founding of the Royal Society of London in 1660, and the publication of Isaac Newton's book: *"Philosophiae Naturalis Principia Mathematica"*. This finally lifted the development of science from its foundations, and it did away with the mythical and magical interpretation of the world. At the same time, "the witch hunt" began throughout the Christian world, which paved the way for abolition of paganism and mysticism, for the esoteric manipulations of consciousness and higher dimensions, instead of the systematic work and knowledge accessible to all. In addition to Euclid's Elements, Newtonian mechanics represents the fundamental crystallization of human awareness in the physical world.

The third event was the birth of the Serbian scientist Nikola Tesla. He completely surpassed Newtonian mechanics and the limiting materialistic view of the world with his research and discovery of limitless energy from ether. He finally found a way to bring light to planet Earth, and enhanced the development of science to such a degree that the rulers of the world had to put a stop to it. He too that he was ahead of his time, so he removed some of his patents, such as wireless power transfer (the Long Island tower) and the direct source of energy from the ether or the energy of "zero point" (electric Pierce-Arrow sedan, 1931). His research into the ether and limitless energy were put aside in favor of the false theories that launched Einstein into popularity of the scientific world.

Tesla claimed that there are speeds far greater than that of the speed of light, and that he had worked with them, which was in accordance with discoveries of quantum physics which in turn suggest that consciousness is at the foundation of nature. This would have brought all of the old viewpoints of social and religious traditions, that then still played a key role, to an end; and human society was not yet ready for this. Consequently, Einstein was used to help launch the lie that nothing could move faster than the speed of light, together with the theory of relativity and the "Big Bang," which played the part of a modern parallel to the obsolete Biblical version of the creation of the world. All of this was concocted and forced upon the world and the scientific public, through the Jesuits and Zionists, to diminish the significance of Tesla's work and hinder scientific development, in order for people and society as a whole to gain more time to prepare themselves for a more gradual pace of development. Indeed, it was not possible for mankind to jump out of the ox cart and into speeds faster than light in the way Tesla generously offered.

Proof that the work of Nikola Tesla was the final turning point of human development on this planet, that man, after detailed comprehension of the material world actualizes the presence of the divine consciousness in this world, can be found in his own words: "The day science begins to study non-physical phenomena (the deeds of the soul's consciousness), it will make more progress in one decade than in all the previous centuries of its existence".

In addition, it was imperative that the ancient knowledge of the human soul and its liberation was kept for the future, and for those mature individuals who always exist, and who are ready to free themselves from the illusions of this world completely through the cycle of reincarnation, irrelevant of historical and sociological development. This was being done in the esoteric schools of Gnostic Christianity and in original Buddhism. These are the only ones who possess the complete unsullied truth of the real nature of the human soul and its liberation.

Before Christ and the linear historical development of human civilization on Earth, negative entities interbred with people and became their rulers. This took place in Babylon, circa 13,000 years ago. All the ruling bloodlines were genetically related, and their genetic uniqueness made them appear outwardly human, although their essence was non-human and was used as a portal through which negative entities could act. They could not show themselves for who they really were because people would recognize them, and when they are recognized they cannot act as they are supposed to. They disguised themselves as human by designing hybrid humans, half human and half non-human; organic portals suitable for possession and used to manipulate the world. The astral world was their natural habitat, and this made it easy for them to influence people who resided in the physical world only.

The hybrids were scarce in number, but they were put in charge of people. Thus, a minority ruled over vast numbers of human beings with ease. All of today's aristocracy and the ruling elite is descended from these hybrids. They moved from ancient Babylon to Rome, and turned the teachings of Jesus into the Christian church, as the crucial factor in binding people's awareness to their senses and physical matter only; to work "by the sweat of your brow", and to learn the basics of knowledge and science. They orchestrated all the coercion and pressure needed to break the inertia of soul's consciousness, in order to make people work and develop the physical world, an endeavor which is the key to acquiring new experiences and possibilities of the divine consciousness in this physical world. After the downfall of Rome, they moved to Venice, and from there to Holland and into all the European courts, then England, and finally the USA.

They are the source of all the negativity in this world, but it's the negativity needed to experience all of the possibilities of divine consciousness, all of the oppositions, all of the experiences that human souls could never have by themselves; they would never be able to agree to or cause such inferior experience.

The symbols of all the rulers (or Illuminati) and their lower executors (the masons) are building tools; their god is "the grand architect of the universe;" they serve Lucifer because he is the consciousness bearer, the bringer of consciousness in matter. Lucifer's characteristic is that he brings the light of consciousness into experiences which souls do not want to touch because of their sublime and divine nature. This world is, to a large degree, such an unfavorable place.

Humans who have known that their soul does not have ties or special interests with this world; to them the physical world is nothing but an illusion, they instead see the presence of the divine consciousness in everything. They see that everything is perfect, and that all possible realities co-exist in parallel. While they are right, such individuals may sit on the ground in primitive cabins for centuries. They are not interested in the development of civilization. However, only via complete civilizational development, from human rights and freedoms, from scientific knowledge of the quantum field, and its use in the sphere of science and technology, can the divine consciousness attain the consciousness of itself, of its essence and the meaning of existence in everything, and all of this through the civilized humans. This is why the coercion and struggle forced upon humans by non-humans and their hybrids is of crucial importance and necessary to overpower the dangerous inertia human souls possess regarding work in this world is the issue.

Make no mistake: a civilized human is the only one who can practically apply awareness of existence within existence itself. The divine consciousness reaches the point of materialization through him. Through the civilized human the divine consciousness expresses itself in the best possible way. Such a civilized human will only be possible in the distant future. Right now, we have just a weak and primitive image of this ideal.

This is the plan for planet Earth; it was created as an elite school for the complete development of awareness of existence through humans, from the transformation of the material world to an awareness of the very nature of matter. To put it more accurately: the Earth was created for the unity of the divine consciousness and existence, in all its detail, from start to finish, through the living experience and actions of man. The development of technology and material culture is planned and intended for planet Earth, and anyone who stands in the way of this will be stopped. Naturally, there are people and civilizations who are not technology-oriented, and who are able to live on their awareness of the divine presence, but they will not be allowed to rule this planet.

It should be emphasized that lack of interest of young souls in the technological progress was justified when there was no technology. Life was much harder then, and people rightfully assumed that this existence equalled prison, and they wanted to escape it and return to their true, higher state. Today, now that technological progress is well under way, many young souls are exhilarated by it and attracted to everything that is new, "urban" and "progressive". However, this interest in many young souls is mostly immature, to a large degree based on using readily available technological advantages rather than the serious work dedicated to their creation, which has always been the characteristic of just a few individuals.

This is the chief reason there are so many conflicts and evil in the world. Evil and violence is bred on the individual plane and in relationships between people due to differing levels of consciousness, lack of understanding, and the human need to experience absolutely anything worth experiencing, mistakes included, not to say "sins". Consciousness is based on the freedom of experience, and this also means the freedom to make a mistake. This is also one of the ways to reach cognition. When the awareness of soul is present in the body to a lesser degree, these people are called young souls, with insufficient maturity acquired from experience of existence in this world.

These people are on the path of learning how to work in the physical world, but some of them are so immature that they do not have enough intelligence to tell good from evil, right from wrong, and since they are more identified with the body and its self-preservational instincts, they find it easy to defend their needs, with violence if necessary. Such immature people are easily possessed by negative astral entities, thus causing all of the hideous crimes and cases of extreme violence found amongst people. They later testify that in those moments they "did not feel like themselves," that they were possessed, that they were unaware of their actions. With the growing experience accumulated over multiple reincarnations, the soul's consciousness becomes ever more present in the body, and together with it the awareness of what is right and what is wrong. It is impossible for people to know what is right and good without awareness of the soul.

On a global scale, similar principles breed similar civilizational conflicts. In the same way that negative astral entities affect immature people and force them to commit individual crimes, the hybrid people and negative entities, Illuminati and aristocracy force entire nations into wars and all-out destruction, whenever a need arises for change and collective progress. One should never forget that wars are the primary instigator of economic and scientific growth. This may be because of the inertia of the material world we live in, due to the principle of dialectics, the unity of opposites that rules it, which inspires people to show their finest virtue in times of greatest stress; too often great good only comes during despicable times.

One good example of this would be in economics. Neither today, not in the near future, is a fair and just economic and financial order likely to happen. Exploitation must exist; there are too many factors that are out of control. Young and immature souls constitute the highest percentage of the population on this planet; if free energy were accessible, they would spend it lavishly on their lower impulses, which would lead to further decay. The same would happen with a just and interest free financial policy.

Economic growth would considerably slow and maybe even stop. There is an inevitability in the fact that the financial order which produces results can only exist for a short time, after which a crisis must be generated which results in a crash, which in turn produces sufficient momentum for a new economic cycle which powers economic growth, albeit for a short time. All of these external coercions are necessary for people with young and immature souls, with an insufficient awareness of the soul within themselves. If they were provided with all the means necessary for the free and unlimited use, it would merely fuel their lower urges, and make them want to lash out and fulfill their immature aspirations. Their lack of consciousness, maturity and inner balance is best expressed in their lack of balance and complacency in the outward environment and in their living conditions.

Illuminati and aristocrats, the owners of all corporations, use various means to put additional pressure on people wherever they can. They poison people through food, medications and vaccines to make people aware of these dangers, to make them health conscious; they twist truth and use media and educational institutions, of which they are exclusive owners, to make them the centers of lies and deceit so that people reach for the truth, and find ways of safeguarding it against the unscrupulous. They make people want to attain real scientific knowledge by testing variables and debunking falseness. In short, their pressure and all their negativity only crystallize the awareness of what is positive in man.

Basically, they simply provoke the opposite, and force people to comprehend the world they live in, step by step. That is all they do. This is a world where opposites rule, and this is the way to make the presence of consciousness stronger. Every man, once they have become aware of their wrongdoing and has asked for repentance, becomes a better man, more aware of the world around him and their role in it. The same thing happens on a global scale with all of mankind. People learn from their mistakes. Apart from the obvious discrepancies, somewhere at the base of such a law is the need of the divine consciousness to experience *everything* that can be experienced. This "everything" should be taken quite literally. It is not an option for an individual to simply accept a truth from some authority and blindly submit to it and follow. Humans must reach the truth on their own, to make awareness of the truth their awareness, and to make the truth their deed. That is the only way to make the consciousness of their soul express the divine consciousness in this world.

Gnostics were the first to point out that **Archons are unable to create, they are merely able to modify what has already been created, to make simulations** (Gnostics called the simulations and simulacrums of Archons "bad copies", the way we would call them virtual reality or the matrix of illusion today). This just means that the Illuminati and all of the negative forces offer options that people choose to realize. No negative force is going to grab someone and throw them off a building or bridge to their imminent death. The force can only lead a man to do it. This is the modus operandi of the Illuminati. They cause the opposing effect, they lead on, they open the door for evil and negativity, and people choose to go through that door; they commit evil because of their lack of knowledge, unconscious of the consequences. *It is in this way that people are made aware of their own unconsciousness; they only materialize human unconsciousness and ignorance.* Thus, the negative entities help man attain a higher level of awareness. Indeed, throughout all of history, people have never before been so aware of this conspiracy as they are today, when it is at its largest, when the coercion and pressure of lies and destruction are greatest.

Global conflicts are mostly based on the opposition of two aspirations. The first is the tendency of soulful people to remain inert, not to do much in the civilizational sense and for the transformation of the material world, and to go back to their divine source, to God and Kingdom come. They rightly feel that the process of materialization is an alien concept to a human soul, but they cannot comprehend that human souls did not arrive in this world just for the sake of discomfort, but to go through it and transform it in accordance with the divine consciousness that they themselves represent, in order to gather all the experiences of existence and take them back to the divine as awareness of itself. Immature aspirations of the return to the divine are present in the ethical religions, like Judaism, Islam and Greek-Orthodox. Likewise, in the old polytheistic and shamanic traditions, there is a tendency towards unity with nature, and through it unity with the divine. Creative work is completely absent.

The second aspiration is in favor of building a material culture as the foundation which enables the perfection of consciousness in matter, and using it as the means to get close to the divine consciousness. Such aspiration exists because consciousness is unable to express itself in the physical world, other than through labor and the transformation of the world. Consciousness possesses the quality of action as well as creation; nothing that exists can be static. In order to gain command of the physical world it must transform it, and make people's lifestyle and the transfer of information between them more efficient, so as to be able to act in the world without impediment. The development of technology and the order of civilization is nothing but what is already present in the quantum field of existence, in which everything is perfect, in which all possibilities co-exist as parallel realities, in which everything is interconnected by instant information transfer which permits accessibility of the consciousness.

An identical concept is expressed here on a large scale, as improving the conditions of life and the possibilities of transport, the accessibility of information via the Internet and mobile broadband. Technological and civilizational improvement is nothing but a manifestation of all the potentials that already exist in the quantum field. Policy that enables human rights and freedoms is nothing but the rule of consciousness among people. These are ways in which the divine consciousness is expressed as sheer existence. There is a spontaneous tendency to turn the potential into concrete, to make implicit (quantum) order explicit. This tendency many call "New World Order," at the forefront of which are the Illuminati with their masons; regrettably they stop at nothing and do not choose their means in achieving their goal, so their overall performance is no better than those who do nothing at all.

There is currently an on-going conflict between the two. The former put spikes in the wheels of civilizational progress and pull backwards, to a return to heaven; they would coolly leave all the land unfarmed. While the latter pull forward, wishing to make a paradise on Earth at all costs, stepping on anything they come across, thus causing even more havoc on planet Earth. It is only owing to the Earth's superior strength and consciousness that life goes on; civilization is making baby steps, developing at a worryingly slow pace.

Life goes on despite the conflicts and chaos all over the globe; people advance with civilizational progress, maybe for the simple reason that the soul's consciousness can never die - it is the sole condition for life. However young or immature it may seem, to people it always conveys the awareness of its true purpose in this world; no matter how lost it may seem it always finds strength. The Earth with its beauty provides additional support.

The ethical religions, Judaism and Islam, hinder the freedom necessary for consciousness to be expressed in all its forms; they dictate everything people may do, thus depriving them of their free will and personal awareness of the proper action. They represent the dictatorship of one-mindedness. Although they were needed for young mankind to cultivate its behavior, through the external coercion of a religious authority, over the course of time they become a burden and restricted the growth of consciousness and the implementation of free will.

The problem is that neither of them are very aware of their nature and the motivation for their actions. Neither of them are familiar with samadhi, the notion that it is necessary for the divine consciousness and existence to merge in the heart of man, and only then will their unity be able to express itself in this world. The more samadhi takes place in man, the more Kingdom come will be on earth, and God's will be done.

Maybe this book can give them the helping hand they so desperately need to meet halfway, for there can be no true civilization without soul's consciousness, nor can soul's consciousness express itself without a true civilization.

***

This was an illustration of how the divine consciousness expresses itself through nature, human society and global development.

Now we shall see how consciousness and existence bind together and are expressed through man themselves.

THE LAW OF NUMBER SEVEN
AND THE SEVEN CHAKRAS

At the beginning, we saw that divine consciousness is expressed as the full spectrum of overall existence. In other words, everything-that-is is always expressed as everything-that-is-possible. The divine consciousness of the Absolute expresses itself in such a manner that it becomes everything that in any way, shape or form can be.

This spectrum may quite appropriately be compared with the spectrum of colors of the sunlight. It breaks up into seven colors through the prism. Sunlight consists of seven colors because the light of divine consciousness is always expressed through the law of number seven, or the seven phases. The principle of seven phases of manifestation is present in everything, not just in light, it is in the sound, hence, the seven notes, and in the process of forming the crystal as well as the realization of many other material processes and events. Nothing is realized following one straight line, every process of realization has its rhythms, oscillations, changes, set backs, additional impulses, and when we take a careful look, we can see that there always are seven of them. The law of number seven is at the foundation of creation. Hence, the Biblical story of the creation of the world in seven days. It is a metaphor which expresses the law of number seven.

Humans are a microcosm, their body is the holographic image of the cosmos in miniature. All the dimensions the cosmos consists of (earth, water, fire, air and ether) are comprised in the human being which gives them the body (earth), feelings and imagination (water), energy and will (fire), thoughts or information (air) and the consciousness itself (ether, the quantum field). Humans are therefore, able to comprehend all the dimensions of the phenomena of nature and to move through all the dimensions. Actually, their "movement" through them is nothing but expanding their focus away from the physical field and on to the higher and wider dimensions. He possesses all of that as their own being. Therefore, "out-of-body" experience and being in higher dimensions is no exit, it is only the expansion of the alertness and consciousness.

The law of number seven, by which the divine consciousness of the Absolute expresses itself as the most general existence, is reflected in man as the microcosm of the overall existence. It is maintained as the system of the psychoenergetic centers otherwise known as chakras.

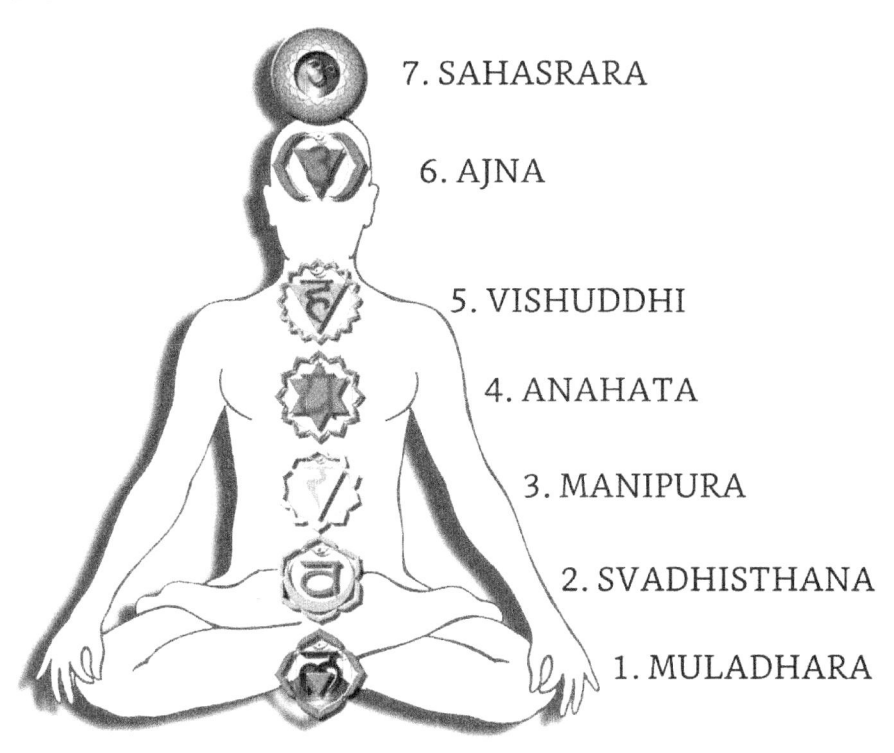

7. SAHASRARA

6. AJNA

5. VISHUDDHI

4. ANAHATA

3. MANIPURA

2. SVADHISTHANA

1. MULADHARA

Chakras are whirls of energy in the form of torus which connect consciousness with existence, through them the consciousness is expressed as existence. The word chakra means whirl or wheel.

Chakras have their colors which are in accordance with the basic colors of the spectrum of sunlight. Chakras are also on the exact location of the glands in the human body, which determine all the hormonal functions as well as functioning of all the vital organs. The glands function under the influence of information body receives from the outside and the inside, mainly via light frequencies, that is colors. DNA molecule is basically a code of light. DNA receives crucial information on how to function from photons, the codes of light of sunlight. Every color of the spectrum of sunlight plays the key role in the functioning of a certain vital organ. That is why there is a healing with colors, and the healing with sun. Pituitary gland is the most important for the functioning of all the remaining glands. The ultraviolet spectrum of sunlight is the key for the functioning of the pituitary gland. Hence, receiving sunlight and colors play the most important part in maintain good health. Body receives sunlight through the eyes at the most. The sunlight, the colors, chakras and the functioning of the vital organs interconnect in one union which gives life.

Every chakra reflects one phase in the process of materialization, from the pure consciousness, ether or the quantum field, from the idea, to the concrete physical realization, the rough material world.

With its seven chakras the human being is a prism which distinguishes the divine consciousness from the existence, and by doing so it joins them, and reveals their original unity.

The fact that the consciousness unites with existence through chakras reveals the reason why every state of consciousness in man is expressed through a correlating event or human conduct. Because of chakras man cannot divide their consciousness from its realization in the existence, every state of consciousness is expressed as behavior of some kind, more accurately, that is the dominant effect of a certain chakra, its energetic influence. And vice versa. Every type of behavior and way of life affect the dominance of a certain chakra. Not only do chakras affect behavior, but behavior also affects the chakras. It is used in yoga practice, by doing certain exercises and behavioral patterns the energy and consciousness are directed to certain chakras and certain aspects of human existence are activated.

In such a manner chakras represent ways of existence, the dominant role of a certain chakra reflects itself in the way we currently exist, what we do and how we perceive reality.

Since the meaning of all the existence is in perception, the divine Absolute experiences the awareness of itself through the existence of cosmos, every individual being is only an individual form through which the divine consciousness actualizes the awareness of itself. Likewise, every chakra in man, as the microcosm, reflects the full spectrum of the possible states of consciousness man is capable of existing with, the full spectrum of perception of the divine consciousness in man and through man. From the most exalted divine state to the lowest animal one, from the complete freedom to the complete conditionality. From the full remembrance of itself, its essence or the soul's consciousness, to the utter oblivion of itself, its essence and the soul's consciousness.

Namely, the system of chakras represents nothing but the spectrum of presence of soul's consciousness in the body.

In the overall existence of man, the issue is none other than the spectrum of the presence of the soul's consciousness in the body.

The soul's consciousness is actually the divine consciousness which is expressed as the existence itself, as our body.

When the consciousness is expressed in the most rudimentary form in the physical body, it is expressed through the first, the lowest chakra, *muladhara*. Once its unity with the existence starts to get more complex, it is expressed through the higher and then a higher chakra. When the consciousness has gathered all the experience of existence to the point it is able to reach awareness of itself in the very existence, or when all the experience of existence crystallizes into the awareness of itself, then the divine soul's consciousness in the human being is expressed through the highest chakra, *sahasrara*.

The highest chakra, *sahasrara*, is the peak the soul's consciousness which can be expressed in the human body. All the chakras are ties of the body with soul, however progressively less pure, while the highest chakra *sahasrara* is the purest bond of body with the soul.

THE DIVISION OF CHAKRAS INTO THREE SECTIONS

A human being has three centers:
1. **Intellectual center** - which determines perception, understanding and expression;
2. **Motoric and instinctive center** - which determines the movement of the body, all autonomous functions and unconscious urges; and
3. **Emotional center** - which is halfway between the above two, and unifies their functioning.

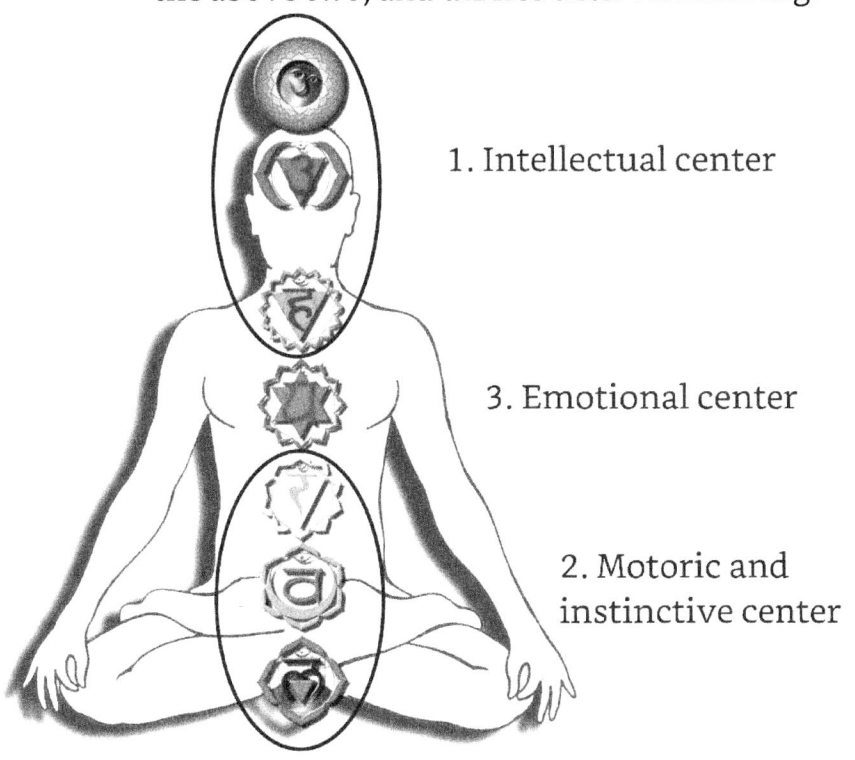

1. Intellectual center

3. Emotional center

2. Motoric and instinctive center

Generally speaking, these three centers represent the merging (3) of the heavenly (1) and the earthly (2) principle in man. The intellectual center represents the principle of freedom and knowledge the motoric center represents everything that conditions and limits us; and the emotional center represents the unifying, understanding and creative surpassing of these opposites.

All of these centers work together, but they are not harmonized if they are not fully realized, so one can outweigh the others.

They blend together. For example, someone may think and feel mechanically, as a force of habit or after being conditioned (the intellectual center may function mechanically when we think formatively), however a greater freedom of choice (which the higher intellectual and emotional centers possess) may help identify and overcome the habits and mechanical behavior of the body and mind.

The emotional center is the most important in unifying the proper functioning of all centers and chakras. It is independent of the body and mind, and for this reason it is able to connect and harmonize them. The emotional center is placed between the intellectual and the motoric.

According to this division, all of the chakras can be divided into three parts, or better yet into two groups: the lower and the upper, with one chakra in between (anahata) that joins them.

The first three chakras (muladhara, svadhistana and manipura) comprise a group that represents the motoric center, mechanical conduct and functioning, the lower being of man, the lower consciousness conditioned by the body and bodily life. They are our link to nature, our ability to survive biologically and in a society. This is the center that people use naturally and spontaneously.

The upper three chakras (vishuddhi, ajna and sahasrara) comprise the intellectual center, through which consciousness conducts understanding, perception and expression. They are our link to the higher mind and the divine soul's consciousness. In order for their functioning to overpower the lower, instinctive center, higher awareness is needed; this can be acquired with karmic maturity and by working on oneself. It is necessary to harmonize the functioning of the lower centers for consciousness to be able to use the higher ones. To harmonize the functioning of the lower centers, it is necessary to conduct consciousness from the higher ones.

The central chakra (anahata) is located in the area of the heart, and it plays a key role in connecting these two groups or centers, in conducting consciousness from the higher to the lower centers. The emotional center is of crucial importance in merging the divine consciousness and existence. The stronger awareness in the center is, the more emotionally mature we are; in other words, the more aware we are of the true nature of everything as the unconditional divine love which makes everything possible, the better the functioning of the remaining chakras, and all the remaining states of consciousness on all the remaining levels.

Therefore, only with the emotional maturity can we judge properly; intellect is not enough, its role is neutral and more directed towards perception. We can make decisions using the motoric center, but they will be aimed at the momentary needs of survival. Only emotional maturity can override these two functions and see everything correctly. Emotional maturity manifests in us first and foremost as unconditional love. Love is the awareness above all opposites, above all limitations, and only this awareness can unite what cannot be united. It can do so because it is the closest to the divine consciousness - itself the source of the unconditional love that makes everything possible.

In order for the divine consciousness to be able to manifest completely in our being, all of the chakras must perform their task properly and not block the flow of energy and consciousness through erroneous functioning. To work properly, they must be properly aligned and harmonized. This correctness can be achieved only through the correct understanding of the nature of existence - knowing that it is a reflection of the divine consciousness in the form of unconditional love which makes everything possible.

Divine consciousness cannot be known in any way in this world, other than in the form of unconditional love in everything, in existence. That is why the key center which unifies everything else is situated in the heart, in the anahata chakra.

Love is the ability to connect things we are unable to connect or understand with our body or mind. Love connects what cannot be connected, comprehends the incomprehensible, and sees the invisible. For this reason, the key chakra is not at the top, but in the center of the human being, in the heart.

It is also important to know that every chakra has its division into a higher, conscious part, and a lower, unconscious and mechanical part. The lower part of every chakra functions mechanically for the sake of survival, because the functioning of every chakra is necessary for the entire being. They can, therefore, function with the minimum of awareness, solely mechanically, and this is when they show their lowest characteristics. In order for consciousness and energy to be sublimated, and with it the quality of being human, it is necessary to strengthen the functioning of the conscious part of every chakra. A chakra's awakening means the awakening of the nature of every method of existence and action represented by that chakra. It is done by making its unaware part more aware. The nature of consciousness is such that one needs to put conscious effort into making it work. Only the unconscious is capable of working of its own accord, in the way nature does. Consciousness strengthens and sublimates itself only through consciousness; an effort that nature does not provide. This is a creative endeavor which can only be based on previous experience of consciousness. This endeavor does not exist anywhere in nature, but only in those individuals making a conscious effort to reach consciousness.

THE HERTZIAN AND NON-HERTZIAN FREQUENCIES OF CHAKRAS

We have previously stated that all of the dimensions of existence originate from ether, or the quantum field. Immediately beyond the ether is the dimension of air, which represents the world of ideas or thoughts in man. This is the information that instigates all physical creation on the lower, rougher planes of existence. These pieces of information are thoughts. Thoughts are ideas or information, owing to which everything exists. Since the world of ideas is the closest to ether or the quantum field in its essence - everything is condensed into oneness, timelessly, together with all the possibilities of existence - all the information regarding any potential existence is timelessly ever present in it. For this reason, we can think about anything we choose: the past, the future, the present, and what has not yet been manifested (and this we call fancy or imagination). This is how in our thoughts, in the world of ideas, we can test all options and combine them in any number of ways, and either arriving at a logical conclusion or making no sense.

Actually, it would be more accurate to say that activities in this world of ideas, the element of air, happen on their own due to proximity with the quantum field ("above"), and the energy of fire ("below"); the presence of soul's consciousness in the physical body makes it happen in the body, specifically in our heads, because sahasrara is in our heads. The presence of the soul makes the activities of the higher dimensions, including the processing of ideas, take place in the body of man. Souls created the physical body in order to unify the phenomena of all the dimensions in one place, and bring them to a higher awareness, in the body of man.

The presence of soul's consciousness gives focus to the phenomena of all ideas moving toward their meaning, understanding of the phenomena, growing awareness, consciousness of itself – which in the long run leads to the divine consciousness that enables everything.

The nature of the quantum field or ether is timeless and spaceless; space and time are constructed in the lower dimensions. Such frequencies of the quantum field are often called non-Hertzian. Hertzian frequencies spread out in space and time. Non-Hertzian, unlike Hertzian, are static; they do not spread out but are self-sufficient, resembling a spherical existence. Such is the nature of the quantum field. It was found to be an unlimited source of energy, and it was named "the zero point", "the energy of the zero point", or "the vacuum energy". This energy was discovered by Tesla, and he named it non-Hertzian to be able to distinguish it from the Hertzian that other scientists work with.

A more detailed technical description is as follows: scalar waves (non-Hertzian) are generated by the interaction of two coherent electromagnetic waves of the same frequency and opposite phase. The resulting energy field created by the opposing electromagnetic fields transforms into the vacuum, into a state of potential, and into the so-called scalar field. The longitudinal wave (Hertzian) is the type of wave where the radiating particles of the medium oscillate in the direction of the wave. It can move only through substantial medium which possess the quality of elasticity. An example of mechanical longitudinal waves are sound waves in air. Electromagnetic scalar waves can be generated by a corresponding modulation of plasmoid structure. In this sense, lightning balls are one specific form of the stationary electromagnetic field. Nikola Tesla not only created them, but he played with them. It was lightning that originally gave him the idea for non-Hertzian frequencies.

To put it plainly, the area of Hertzian waves is the area below the speed of light. This is the area we are able to perceive with our senses and our physical mind. The area of non-Hertzian waves exceeds the speed of light it is actually instantaneous. This is the area physicists have discovered as the nature of the quantum field, in which a particle can exist as both a particle and a wave, and which is entirely subject to the awareness and perception of the conscious viewer. This area we are unable to perceive with our senses and the physical mind, but we can access it with our inner senses and our higher mind. Tesla was not short of the latter!

Therefore, the source of thoughts or ideas, the element of air, is non-Hertzian: static, spheric and complete. This is why thoughts are so close to the timeless present, and this is why they can transcend space and time. Thoughts actually represent the compression of information of absolutely everything in space and time, independently of space and time. They can be this because they are the closest to ether or the quantum field.

They are at the top of the structure of human being, as the highest chakra, sahasrara. As such, this chakra is most profoundly non-Hertzian in nature; it is beyond space and time, above human body.

The thicker and more solid space and time get their conditioning and functioning through the lower chakras, where more Hertzian functioning is expressed. The frequency of every lower chakra is correspondingly more Hertzian.

NON-HERTZIAN FREQUENCIES
OF THE QUANTUM CONSCIOUSNESS

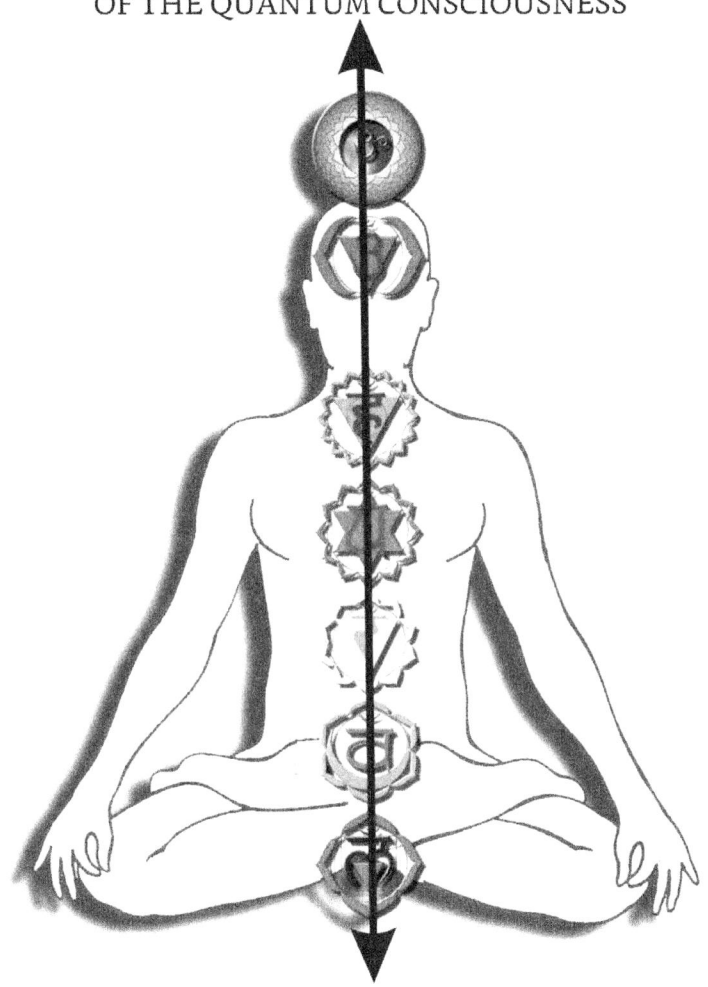

HERTIAN FREQUENCIES OF THE 3D PHYSICAL WORLD

The lowest chakra, *muladhara*, is the most Hertzian in its frequency. Consciousness is the most exposed to the opposing factor of physical survival in this chakra, with a prevailing illusion of materiality and linear space and time where the subject feels alienated.

In other words, the frequency of the first chakra is the lowest, and the frequency of the seventh is the highest.

The characteristic of the lower frequencies is materialism, and of the higher chakras – spirituality.

The first and the last chakra represent the ultimate polarization of existence, pure consciousness (*sahasrara*) and the most concrete existence (*muladhara*) - which does not need consciousness or sense, is just natural causality. Our spine, with the complete system of chakras, is like a lever magnetized to opposite poles, where the highest, sahasrara, consists of non-Hertzian frequencies, and the first, muladhara, consists of Hertzian ones.

This explains why our consciousness can have both the experience of timeless presence (non-Hertzian nature of the quantum field) and the experience of the solid materiality of linear time, trapped by causality (the nature of Hertzian frequencies). You can be completely blinded by the sensory, material world (*muladhara*), or experience transcendental pure awareness (*sahasrara*), or be somewhere in space and time, moving along the lines of those two extremes.

Chakras represent all the possibilities of the experience of existence, from the most rudimentary and conditioned, to pure awareness of itself, of the sense of existence, of the unity of the divine consciousness, which is free to manifest itself in all ways.

This opposite polarization of the human being, between the first and the last chakras, enables the flow of energy through man. Humans would not have the energy needed for life if not for this polarization along their system of chakras. Hence, the energy man uses in their life and work is always connected to the state of their consciousness. The system of chakras is called the psychoenergetic system for this reason.

Since the divine consciousness expresses itself into existence according to the model of the holograph, where every tiny detail contains the principles of the whole, the same is true in chakras; the polarization of all the chakras from Hertzian to non-Hertzian frequencies reflects not only on the entire system of chakras (from the first to the last), but on each one separately. Every chakra itself is polarized into Hertzian and non-Hertzian frequencies, and the energy of every chakra moves in the shape of a torus: rotating from the center outward, then back again.

This further enables dynamics and the ability to grow and transform, to transfer energy from one to another, as well as the constant energy communication between all the chakras.

POLARIZATION OF OPPOSITES IN CHAKRAS

UNITY

OPPOSITES

The polarization of chakras does not exist just in the nature of their frequencies, but in the relationship between consciousness and existence. The full spectrum of chakras, from the first down to the last, represents one big polarization between consciousness and existence, between conscious and unconscious, matter and spirit, awareness of unity with the divine whole, and split consciousness, alienated from the whole.

Actually, all of the chakras together represent the transition from the Hertzian to the non-Hertzian frequencies of existence in seven stages.

In the highest chakra, sahasrara, the awareness of unity is completely present because here existence is non-Hertzian. As the consciousness descends into existence, through the lower chakras, it becomes increasingly more polarized, following the principle of opposites; it becomes more and more exposed to rougher conditions, and vulnerable to bigger presence of opposites. In the lowest chakra, muladhara, consciousness exists in the form of Hertzian frequencies and for that reason it is the most sensory; consciousness is completely polarized into opposites because it's the furthest away from its source, the divine soul's consciousness. The main characteristic of existence at this point is a lack of awareness of itself, exposed to the unconscious causality and conditionality of events.

It is often said that only urges and instincts prevail here. Struggle for survival at all costs - even at the cost of other people's lives - is the dominant feature. It can be said that due to the maximum polarization in the lowest chakra, life has been reduced to absurdity. Although all energy originates from this point, life can turn into its own opposite because human lack of awareness making them oblivious to the life around him; thus, the functioning of this chakra drives him to kill to survive. The functioning of the first chakra is equally life-giving and life-taking. In this way, the opposition of the functioning of the first chakra is emphasized. It is the root of all suffering and the downfall of man, as much as it is the source of life.

Because of this, Buddha said the cause of all suffering is in the drive for life.

Every higher chakra represents an increasingly elevated awareness of existence, an increasingly elevated recognition of the identical divine consciousness present in all existence, and therefore an increasingly elevated propensity for expressing unconditional love. Consciousness ascends to a higher chakra by becoming aware of the true nature of the lower chakra. Every chakra represents a level of awareness, an outlook on the world, on reality. When the world is viewed with a strong identification with one chakra only, it is very hard to resist subjectivity and one-sidedness. The lower the chakra, the stronger this identification. Identification of consciousness in chakras is necessary for their proper functioning; the energy moves centripetally in them to sustain functioning of the chakra.

Owing to the fact that a human being possesses multiple chakras, they can transcend their subjectivity, compare various levels and states of consciousness, and strengthen their objective awareness. Objective awareness is not situated in any center or chakra, or in any specific state of consciousness, but in the experience of change in states of consciousness through all the centers. The awareness of unity in the highest chakra cannot exist without the experience of opposites from all the lower centers.

THE HIGHER AND LOWER NATURE OF CHAKRAS

One of the most obvious characteristics of chakras is their vertical alignment. Each one is higher than the previous one. This is no coincidence. The vertical positioning of the chakras shows us the nature of energy flow and its association with the states of consciousness. The essence of man is connected to the way he looks and the way he moves. Unlike all other beings, man is upright, and this fact is not merely a result of the evolution of movement, but is closely associated with the focusing of consciousness and energy, and with movement from the lower to the higher form of existence. All of this reflects the position of the chakras.

The polarization explained previously must somehow be expressed in three-dimensional space. The nature of the polarization of consciousness and energy is such that in three-dimensional space it is expressed as low, down, conditioned, hard or negative, and as high, exalted, easy or positive. The positive frequencies are "high" and the negative "low". In our experience, everything that is negative, and what works to condition, is low and down, and everything that is positive and exalted is up. Paradise is in heaven, and hell is under the ground.

Consciousness is in its essence unconditioned and all-embracing, and in existence it is always expressed as a tendency to attain a higher level of freedom and unconditionality - and the surpassing of conditionality, or transcendence. Hence, all of existence is moving in the direction of greater knowledge and awareness of itself. This is expressed in existence as the gradual improvement of functions, the evolution of living beings through motion, action and perception, and the improvement of human work and quality of life. With fine, cultured manners we sublimate the consciousness and energy to higher levels.

Every chakra is higher than the previous one, and it owes its position to its meaning in relation to the lower chakra. ***Every chakra represents one more expression of higher consciousness than the lower chakra; one victory over the lower state of consciousness.*** We can recognize this with experience. Every time we surpass some state that represented the lower, conditioned consciousness, the transcendence we experience is a true sublimating. Our previous conduct, which was under the influence of the consciousness of the lower chakra, seems to us from our newly gained perspective as almost alien - as though some other lower beings were responsible, not us. We can observe from above, more objectively, our previous behavior (lower chakras), and are in awe at how we could have done something so low, negative and limiting.

Such insight enables differentiation of the higher states of consciousness; we can say that the chakra alignment, from the lower to the higher, assists us in differentiating the consciousness of each chakra. We can attain objective consciousness of each chakra only from the higher perspective, when we rise from one level to the next.

All of human culture is based on this sublimating of consciousness, from the urge and unconscious drive of the lower chakras to higher, more aware conduct.

The principle of sublimating of consciousness according to the chakra system is connected with the activity principle of consciousness itself, and with energy. When it moves downward, energy decreases; when it moves in the direction of the higher chakras, the energy level increases. This motion corresponds with the states of consciousness. When we are occupied with the conditioning of the lower centers, we lose energy and our consciousness is low, negative and conditioned. When we surpass the unconscious conditionality of the lower urges and mechanical conditioning of our actions, we have more energy and more objective awareness.

The nature of the chakra's impact is such that they connect the consciousness in the body with energy. We cannot have consciousness without energy. A higher level of energy is a necessary condition for higher consciousness. Because of the way consciousness and energy are connected to one another, we cannot use our energy in one way, hoping to achieve certain goals, and remain aware in a different way, with different goals. In other words, we cannot be servants of sin and of righteousness simultaneously; we need to choose which chair to sit on. We cannot do one thing with another on our mind. Actually, we can, but doing so wastes both our time and energy, and deceives the consciousness.

Energy is a phenomenon that follows the consciousness; or better yet, a phenomenon which is induced by the very presence of consciousness. In our body it moves upwards and downwards, from one chakra to another, from greater conditionality to less, and from ignorance to cognition.

The vertical position of the chakras, and man themselves, has to do with the earth's magnetism and the laws of physical attraction, and the conditioning of the consciousness. In the vertical position, every chakra relies gravitationally on the lower one; every lower chakra protects the higher, by serving as its foundation - thus exposing higher chakras to less gravitational pull, which facilitates their elevation. In the horizontal position, every chakra is equally exposed to the earth's gravity and physical conditioning. For this reason, being horizontal is a passive position, adequate for sleeping only. An upright posture is the only correct position for meditation, and the only proper state for awareness - that is, for activating the energy and awareness from the lowest to the highest chakra. Even a stooped posture reflects a blockage in the movement of energy and consciousness, the negative state.

To be able to understand this better we must remind ourselves that gravity is an electrostatic phenomenon of huge proportions. Planets, and all the celestial bodies, are electromagnets which induce life energy with their movement. Life energy is also induced between the earth and the ionosphere. All of nature is designed to be the stage for these dynamic electromagnetic relationships. The chakras in us are nothing but small holographic models of this gigantic electromagnetic cosmic phenomenon.

Therefore, we can clearly see the nature of the frequency of the three groups of chakras, which we have determined to be motoric or mechanical, emotional and intellectual. Every phenomenon is based on the corresponding frequencies. The lowest group, the first three chakras, in charge of mechanical behavior, consists of the lowest frequencies. The three top chakras that constitute the intellectual center, consist of the higher and finer frequencies.

The characteristics of the lower frequencies are agony and fear, narrowing of consciousness, identification, conditionality and addiction, and everything connected with materialism. These are the characteristics of the first three chakras that function spontaneously in the majority of people.

The characteristics of the high or fine frequencies are freedom and clarity of perception, and a higher presence of consciousness, positive feelings and frankness. These are the characteristics of the top three chakras (5,6 and 7).

The negative Archon forces that rule this world base their dominance on strengthening the focus on the first three chakras, and use this to control human behavior They increase the functioning of the lower center by narrowing consciousness and perception, and limiting them to the material aspects of life (this is often done through the media and education); thereby forcing people to live in constant fear and struggle for survival (by inducing perpetual warfare, as well as economic instability and dependence).

The fact of frequencies is simple: the one we choose to emphasize is the one we live with. The nature of the frequency modulates our perception. By changing our frequency, we change our perception, and with it the reality we are in. However, the nature of every frequency is momentary and therefore prone to change; in other words, it is always virtual, it is based on freedom. Consciousness can always change every frequency, every perception and reality. The only requirement for change is to have enough awareness, and with it enough energy.

Therefore, if we live in a virtual reality which keeps conditioning us, and amply supported by the negative Archon forces, then all we have to do is to change the frequency - to change our state of consciousness. This is always possible because it is already in us.

Soul's consciousness is our essence, and not any specific frequency of any chakra.

Various frequencies of various chakras are merely caught in the whirlpool of the soul's consciousness, and are dazzled by it, and so identify temporarily with the states characterized by the frequencies of experienced phenomena. It would be more accurate to say that the divine consciousness of our soul orchestrates the whole affair. It is all part of its hide-and-seek game to reveal all its possibilities, everything it in its essence represents.

THE FUNDAMENTAL NATURE AND THE MEANING OF EVERY CHAKRA

Chakras represent the seven basic phases in which consciousness and existence merge and manifest.

That is why there are seven different levels of consciousness and existence in man, which the yoga system of chakras best depicts as:

1) Deep sleep without dreams (*muladhara*)
2) Dreaming (*svadhisthana*)
3) Average daily experience of being awake (*manipura*)
4) Testifying of the previous three (*anahata*)
5) Mental awareness of the divine consciousness (*vishuddhi*)
6) Enabling the body to allow the transcendental divine consciousness to actively and directly participate in existence (*ajna*), and
7) The complete openness of the being to the presence of the divine soul's consciousness; the disappearance of any identification with objective existence, due to the complete openness to the presence of the divine soul's consciousness; that is, the disappearance of any difference between existence and the divine consciousness that enables it (*sahasrara*).

The first level is a state of pure existence, as is the seventh, but the first is unaware of itself while the seventh is completely aware of itself and its unity with existence.

It goes without saying that the seventh level is the only one that truly matches reality, while all the others express different levels of unconsciousness of reality, and the gradual process of becoming aware of reality. All of the dynamics and versatility of existence are expressed through these processes of awareness.

The first three levels or states of consciousness (deep sleep, dreams, and the state of being awake) correspond with the first three chakras: *muladhara, svadhisthana* and *manipura*. Most people act naturally with them, which means they do so without any spiritual culture or willful intention. They can be recognized as urges (the first), desires (the second) and the desire for power (the third chakra). The fourth chakra (*anahata*) corresponds with the fourth state of consciousness, or the first temporary experiences of transcendental consciousness, the consciousness of unity with the divine consciousness in the existence itself.

The fifth chakra (*vishuddhi*) corresponds with the fifth state of consciousness, in which transcendental consciousness consolidates as a steady consciousness, but on the level of knowledge and its expression only, not as the entire being. It reflects the mental understanding of consciousness and existence. The sixth chakra (*ajna*) corresponds with the sixth state of consciousness, in which transcendental soul's consciousness permanently unveils in the whole being, and pure and complete perception of the divine consciousness in existence occurs This is the type of perception one cannot describe with thoughts, as it surpasses the mind. The seventh chakra (*sahasrara*) corresponds with the seventh state of consciousness, which represents the highest presence of the divine consciousness in the body and the physical world in general.

1. *Muladhara*

Muladhara is the first or the root chakra. It connects us to the pure energy of nature, the energy of planet earth. For that reason, it is located in the crotch area. Our body receives all the vital energy for life from this chakra, in the most elementary sense: whole and unpolarized. We get our instinct for survival from it in its most original form. Its color is dark red. In its functioning it is neutral; it supports and gives strength to everything its energy is invested in. It contains the primordial energy of nature, a *shakti*, called *kundalini*. Its very name indicates the fact that it exists like a "curled up snake"; or in other words, as potential waiting to develop through higher centers, by uniting itself with consciousness and awareness.

Outside of man the principles of this chakra express pure nature, vital energy which gives life to everything without exception. However, this should not be understood naively, because the energy for manifestation is received by both positive and negative phenomena. This chakra in its negative aspect expresses the loss of energy, which in the human experience means death and destruction of life in all its forms. The annihilation of life is the negative side of this chakra; its energy is completely unconscious, and therefore it is capable of destroying life even in an effort to save it at all costs. One simple example of this is when a person, limited to the functioning of this chakra, eats too much food out of a desire for more energy, in order to live and survive, but they're actually doing the exact opposite – killing themselves with food, growing progressively more unhealthy. Another example of the negative functioning of this chakra is shamelessly taking life energy in all available ways, often in a destructive manner.

Due to its neutrality, together with the influence of other planets, the most corresponding influence on this chakra is Mercury.

2. Svadhisthana

Svadhisthana is the second chakra, placed above the first, in the region of the sexual organs. The original vital energy from the first chakra is for the first time polarized for the purpose of giving birth to new forms of life. It is the source of sexuality and of all the ways we exchange energy with other people and with our surroundings. Because of this energy exchange, it is the source of all joy connected with body, usually expressed through sexuality; but also, the opposite of joy - hatred, anger and cruelty. So, it is the source of all conflicts and violence towards life. Since the svadhisthana chakra has a dual nature, in a man with a low level of consciousness, sexuality is always associated with violence and hate. It is far from the source of consciousness and objective knowledge (the sixth and the seventh chakras), and in close proximity to the first chakra, the pure energy where the imperative is to survive; consciousness in the second chakra is expressed as the principle of complacency in every way. In translation its name means "in its own center". Consciousness expressed through this chakra justifies and rationalizes any action that relates to the principles of pleasure and survival, from love to hate.

The first two chakras have the greatest energetic pull; they are, in terms of energy, the strongest in man. The first chakra manifests its power in the struggle for survival and maintaining the life of body in every possible way. The second chakra manifests its power and attraction through the struggle for survival, too, but in the exchange of sex. It is only logical that life energy is expressed in this way first. Sexuality is a strong force, because it must be for beings to keep multiplying and for the species to survive.

In sexuality we feel as full of life as possible (because this chakra is the closest to the source of life energy, the first chakra). Consciousness itself does not possess the instinct for multiplying, because it is as omnipresent as the origin of existence. It is necessary for the power of beings, materially and in energy, to be stronger than the consciousness, so that the instinct for reproduction survives. This strength is justified, but due to its low position and distance from the source of consciousness (the seventh chakra) it is exposed to a big polarization: the law of opposites. Therefore, it is often linked with the negation of life in all its forms, and most of all in sexuality with all destructiveness and violence. Sexuality that creates life is the source of the greatest pleasure in this world, but it has always been hand-in-hand with perversions, and twisted life.

Because of the lack of objective consciousness, and the proximity of the life energy source, sexual pleasure can be found in almost anything: within the same sex, with objects, even with animals. All it takes is to experience this type of pleasure, and it will become an obsession, grounded with rational explanations and justifications. The mind on the level of the second chakra always justifies its actions when following the principle of pleasure.

For this reason, sexuality has always been the biggest challenge to the presence of consciousness in existence. It is a very powerful tool for the transformation of energy of the lower being (the first three chakras) into higher forms of existence, via the science of tantra; but, at the same time, due to its power it has always been the primary cause of the decline of soul's consciousness in the body, and all the associated consequences.

Outside man, in the world, the principle of the second chakra is manifested in everything that Eros represents: in all the shapes of beauty and pleasure, from flowers to birds twittering - birds whose singing has the sexual function of multiplying - and in the beauty of people, and all human activities which relate to beauty and fun in all its forms. Even from the darkest places, where people experience the lowest passions with all their negative consequences, but which are always justified and rationalized (most often as human rights and liberties) while in reality they are nothing but licentiousness. This chakra is directly responsible for licentiousness being wrongly interpreted as freedom, and a very desirable belief that it, although it brings nothing but the loss of energy through the activities of this chakra.

Due to the principle of complacency this chakra, together with the influence of other planets, astrologically best fits the profile of Venus. Its color is orange.

3. *Manipura*

The third chakra is *manipura*, or "the city of jewels". It is located above the navel. Unlike the first and second chakras, which get their energy from the earth completely raw (*muladhara*), and in a state of basic polarization (*svadhisthana*), the energy here is received from the cosmos, from the wider whole. For this reason, it is used in far more versatile ways and with a much higher level of awareness. Unlike the functioning of the first two chakras, which is limited to the body and the instinct for survival and the polarization of energy through sexuality and the principle of joy, for the first time here energy is used for something else; it has other goals that are not concerned with the body and its survival, but instead with human society and other beings - the wider concept. This energy is united and used for people's mutual benefit and general well-being. From this point onwards, consciousness begins to create a more cultured lifestyle that is not solely conditioned by personal actions and reactions. Consciousness builds culture and civilization in this sphere. Hence its title, which refers to "the city of jewels" or the perfect city.

Humans who have used their consciousness to surpass the first two chakras become a creator in other fields of life now, as they are not just perpetually nurturing their physical body. Here they develop an awareness of the wider community and the interests of society. While they were using the energy of the first two chakras for their survival and personal sexual pleasure, they use the energy from the third chakra for higher goals; above all, for the prosperity and survival of their family, for creating offspring and getting married, as well as taking an active role in the life of the community, who share the same set of values.

Outside man, in the world, it can be said that the divine consciousness created all civilization and material culture by means of the third chakra, with all the struggle and perseverance necessary for such an accomplishment.

Therefore, because of the effort to rise above the first two chakras, together with the influence of the other planets, astrologically this chakra most appropriately corresponds with Mars. Its color is yellow.

4. *Anahata*

The first three chakras represent the lower group of chakras, the instinctive or the motoric center. This center (comprised of the first three chakras) is in charge of movement and functioning of consciousness in the physical body.

When awareness of the mind itself gains enough power, the fourth level of consciousness appears as intuitive overcoming of the first three, and the ability to testify about them. The first three levels are provided by nature, and for their everyday functioning nothing is required; letting go is enough, since they are all that's required for natural survival, in most cases. Because of this simple fact most people reside in them their entire life, with only rare and short elevations to the fourth level of consciousness, usually induced by some emotional trauma, or a powerful imagination. The permanent realization of the fourth level is the outcome of disciplined spiritual practice and dedicated effort to overcome the gravity of natural survival and the first three states. (Such spiritual discipline is found in the Buddhist practice of contemplation, *zazen*, *satipatthana* and *dhyana*). Its function is not previously determined by nature and is allowed to a small number of individuals only, because for the survival of organic life it is necessary for the majority of people to be conditioned by the spontaneous reproduction found on the first three levels.

One of the chief characteristics of the fourth level of consciousness is that, due to the practice of contemplation and occasional experience of pure, transcendental awareness of oneself, or consciousness of all notions and of the body itself, suddenly the experience of being awake during sleep takes place; more accurately the first out-of-body experiences start to happen. This is a transitional state and relates to the beginning of the practical work on awakening. It corresponds with the activation of the fourth chakra, anahata. The first experiences of unity with the divine consciousness take place here. With the first out-of-body experience, the first experience of unity with the divine appears. They are always followed by utter and complete love and bliss toward all existence, in any way, shape or form, because awareness of the divine cannot be experienced otherwise - it is the unconditional love that makes everything possible.

If work on oneself proves to be successful, the fifth state of consciousness surfaces, in which man finally distinguishes between their own alertness and the unconscious conditionality of natural phenomena. Being awakened, he now sees all of nature as one unique whole and, because of this insight, they recognize their own freedom and independence (*kaivalya*) from that whole, from what is happening. He sees nature as a unique whole because they themselves have become unique and whole; they have become the personification of such a reality, since now being awakened they are able to recognize it - it takes one to know one. Materiality disappears and spirituality emerges as the only perspective, now perfectly clear and which causes love and bliss (*ananda*).

All of this is the description of the fourth chakra, anahata. The word in translation means "unimpaired", which indicates wholeness, the first experience of the whole consciousness of oneself and the objective reality we get from the higher intellectual center, the top three chakras. Its name also means "unhurt," which points to the overcoming of suffering which is characteristic of the first three levels of existence or chakras; more accurately this is known as bliss, as the most direct experience of unconditional love, which is the only objective reality.

The symbol of this chakra is a hexagram, two triangles set in opposite positions, one pointing downward and the other pointing upward. The triangle pointing downward represents the soul's consciousness which descends into the body, the matter; and the triangle pointing upward represents the sublimating of an awakened existence toward the divine soul's consciousness. Therefore, it is a very appropriate symbol of merging and uniting the higher and the lower centers in this chakra.

The love which man is capable of is just a tiny reflection of the unconditional divine love which enables existence, love that is the divine consciousness itself, whose tiny part we use as our own consciousness. Every time we grow closer to objective reality, we are unable to distinguish this consciousness from an unconditional love for everything; we are unable to experience it in any way but as unconditional love for everything. Actually, only such love can bring us this consciousness. They always go together. The merging of consciousness and existence happens as the emanation of the unconditional divine love.

That is why their unity is placed in the heart of man, in the chakra *anahata*, between the source of consciousness and the source of existence.

The principle of consciousness moving along chakras is as follows: it descends from the highest chakra to the lowest, from the soul to matter and the physical body; in this way, with its own presence, consciousness attracts energy to express itself in ever more complex and exalted ways, through the higher chakras. With its own presence consciousness lifts energy upward; in every chakra there is a unity of consciousness and energy, in accordance with the nature of chakra.

All it takes to conduct consciousness to the lowest chakra, and enable life energy from the first chakra to lift to the higher centers and chakras, to finalize the unity of consciousness and existence, is to set the functioning of all the chakras properly, because proper unity of consciousness and energy cannot happen with dysfunctioning chakras. To properly harmonize chakra functioning means to understand their functioning and the principles of their functioning. We can comprehend everything fully only from the central point, anahata chakra, which unites the higher and the lower group.

Consciousness and energy actually constantly circulate through all the chakras and through the whole body, from top to bottom. All that's needed is to become aware of it, to understand the functioning of every center, the way it works, and why it works the way it does, and that is possible only if we surpass the consciousness of the lower chakra with the consciousness of the higher chakra.

Therefore, chakra activation and the rising of kundalini from the first chakra cannot be achieved by merely repeating mantras. It can only be achieved with a deeper understanding of the way we exist through every individual chakra, by expressing awareness of existence through every single chakra. In this way, consciousness acts of its own accord, by rising *kundalini* in the only correct way. Any artificial attempt made, for example by using some exercises, can only increase the power of the unconscious. To give more energy to the unconscious and ignorance is a recipe for disaster. Many people have experienced the spontaneous awakening of *kundalini*, sometimes induced by circumstances, but the upsurge of energy into higher centers or chakras was not followed with greater understanding and awareness. Thus, these people experienced a wider perception without understanding what it entails. Such people fall victims to disturbed behavior and a perception they fail to grasp. Psychiatric clinics are packed full of these people.

When human growth is at stake, consciousness is first and last in importance. The disruption in the functioning of any chakra is only possible because of a lack of awareness; or more accurately, its due to the disruption in harmony between consciousness and energy (the way we exist, act).

Outside man, the principle of the *anahata* chakra is manifested as the divine love which enables everything. It manifests in the world in human goodness and unconditional love, in deeds of love, through the man who has become aware of the divine existence, or existence as the divine consciousness.

Due to the magnitude and significance of this chakra, together with the influence of the other planets, this chakra is best described by the astrological influence of Jupiter. Its color is green.

5. *Vishuddhi*

The activation of the fifth chakra, *vishuddhi*, is characterized by the ability to express the nature of reality in thought and verbal form, as an awareness of unity. This expression is the highest level of understanding which can be achieved, both in thoughts and words.

The ability to understand everything (*anahata* chakra) goes with the ability to express our understanding. Actually, only once we successfully express a certain state of consciousness or the way of existence, we have successfully comprehended it. The name of this chakra means purification; it brings the final cleansing of all impurities and ambiguity.

Through this chakra existence expresses itself in all forms of communication, in the process of joining the meaning and sense of things, from language and writing, to science and art. Here we finally distinguish between sense and meaning, the revelation of truth. This means that the negative aspect of this chakra is its hiding. Through this chakra the world of ideas acts as the inspiration for action, will is expressed in both words and thoughts. Hence, this chakra is important for the functioning of the mind or thoughts, for the culture of thought, and all the ways of expressing energy in general.

Due to the thorough distinguishing between right from wrong, and the purification of everything erroneous, this chakra, together with the other planets, is best associated with the influence of Saturn. Its color is blue.

6. *Ajna*

If the fifth chakra is complete expression, the sixth chakra, ajna, is complete perception. Consciousness in this chakra perceives what the senses (using the senses for perception is the job of the first three chakras) cannot, and the sixth chakra may have this supernatural perception thanks to emotional maturity (the fourth chakra), and the ability to express this maturity (the fifth chakra). Without these preconditions the sixth chakra cannot be used; is not possible to use any shortcuts in order "to activate the third eye", the sixth chakra.

Proper insight into reality is possible only when the functioning of the first three chakras is harmonized, when they are tuned; in other words, when the functioning of the motoric and the instinctive centers are awakened (which means that consciousness gains superiority), when at the center of emotional maturity, the functioning of the higher and the lower centers is harmonized, and consequently can be adequately expressed (the fifth chakra). Only then is it possible to activate the sixth chakra or "the third eye"; only then is it possible to perceive reality correctly. In addition, as every higher chakra is activated by surpassing the lower one, or more precisely by awakening the function of the lower one, when one reaches the principle of objective consciousness of the lower chakra, one replaces the instinctive principle for survival.

The position of this chakra points to its connection with the pineal gland, which secretes dimethyltryptamine (DMT), which acts as the molecular link with higher consciousness. DMT is set for accepting the consciousness of the higher mind in the body. Depending on its ability to accept the vibrations of the higher consciousness, it further causes the secretion of the neurotransmitter serotonin and the hormone melatonin, which regulates further physiological processes in accordance with the acceptance of the presence of the higher consciousness in the body by the lower or the physical mind. This is the physiological explanation of why this chakra is placed in the center of the head, behind the eyes, and why it is called "the third eye". The real meaning of its name is "know" or "obey".

The clearer understanding of its physiological impact gives us its link to sunlight. The pineal gland is connected to the eyes, through which it receives UV radiation from the sun. UV radiation is of key importance for the functioning of this gland, and via the pineal gland for the functioning of the entire immune system, and our health.

Photons that come from the sun are actually light codes; this gland receives information crucial for our existence via the sun's radiation. Since our DNA is basically a form of light code, it is a process through which our DNA receives information and is able to stay alive, using the sun's rays. The sun is, in reality, the light of the divine consciousness, the radiation of the soul's consciousness on a far higher level than that which is incarnated in the human body. In this way, the soul's consciousness in the body merges with the soul's consciousness on a far higher, cosmic level, via sunlight (light codes, photons) via the pineal gland.[11]

This chakra is associated with the notion of *chittakasha* in the science of *yoga*. It is the space of consciousness or the mind; more accurately, the space (*akasha*) which enables everything can become directly mentally known (*chitta*), the world of ideas or thoughts joins (air) with *akasha* (the quantum field). If the fifth chakra (*vishuddhi*) is mental expression, speech and word, here it is consciousness that goes beyond thoughts. Therefore, we awaken this chakra and fully activate it when we are witnesses to our thoughts, to the whole mind.

Consciousness is the closest to the quantum field in *ajna*, therefore it possesses the purest consciousness that can exist in the body, the consciousness which is the closest to the quantum mind, the field that everything emanates from and everything belongs to. The name *ajna* also means "command", because consciousness from this chakra has the power to create; thoughts are directly materialized in reality. For this reason, this chakra is tied

---

[11] One may easily draw the obvious conclusion here of how truly harmful sunglasses are, both to eyesight, and health, but especially to mental health.

to the manifestation of superpowers (*siddhi*). Nature is obedient to man when he acts from this chakra.

Since consciousness detects in this chakra what cannot be detected by the normal senses, independently of space and time, this chakra is best defined by the astrological influence of the planet Uranus. Its color is purple.

7. *Sahasrara*

When man perceives reality for what it is, they are no longer conditioned by nature, because it has already achieved its purpose; they have surpassed everything that ties him to the being and time, and they have become a place of opening toward the soul's consciousness which enables existence. It is the state of this awareness where any individuality and corporeality are barely noticeable, because the complete and permanent awakening is the direct expression of the unity of each human with the whole; more accurately, unity with the divine consciousness which enables existence in its entirety.

This complete alertness indicates complete participation in the entire existence, but at the same time, it denotes complete independence of existence. A different form of alertness is not possible, because it is unity with the transcendental Absolute, which is at the same time human essence. Therefore, a man having recognized their unity with it, ceases to be different from it, in the same way that water does not differ from water while being in water, air from air, light from light. It all represents the seventh chakra, *sahasrara*, which is at the top of the head. It is placed just a little above the top of the head, denoting its transcendental nature, its independence of the body. Its name means "a thousand fold", which means that it is infinite and unconditioned. Its color is white.

This is the higher mind of man, the higher consciousness that makes man aware of everything in existence. This higher consciousness man has as the bond with their own soul; it is the soul's consciousness which has not yet embodied itself, but has stayed close enough and kept its independence from the body and bodily mind, in order to be the guarantee for man's awakening and awareness of themselves, and of their transcendental soul. It becomes completely awakened only with the complete awakening of the functioning of the lower chakras; when we are objectively aware of every form of existence, of the nature of every action, of our whole being, and that means completely independent of everything.

The transcendental nature of this chakra, which is represented with its position just a little above the top of the head, signifies its independence from the body, from the being and from existence. The essence of consciousness is in its independence from the being, that is why it is said that it surpasses or transcends it. Owing to this fact, consciousness can make every phenomenon of being fully aware. If the consciousness were on the same level as the being, or in unity with it, there could never be an objective consciousness about the whole being and every phenomenon. "Objective" means "independent", but at the same time it means "true". These three notions are one and the same in the meaning of consciousness.

Consciousness loses its objectivity and veracity to the exact degree that it is identified with the being. The identification of consciousness brings all the problems of human existence, all the problems of incarnation of the soul in the body, all the problems of ignorance (avidya) as the cause of all suffering, and all human and life dramas, and all of karma as well.

This chakra is the source of soul's consciousness in man. Without it, people would be just highly developed animals. In most people it may be inactive, or very slightly active, mostly through activities that do not get recognized as its activities - through intuition and creative imagination, dreams. It can have its outward influence, but also an inward impact; more often than not it acts indirectly, through synchronicity in the chain of events.

Due to the nature of this chakra, very often it is unrecognized or unclear to people, although it represents openness for soul's consciousness and for the divine consciousness. This chakra is best defined by the astrological influence of the planet Neptune.

THE PRINCIPLES OF CHAKRA FUNCTIONING IN THE WORLD AND HISTORICAL DEVELOPMENT

The functioning of the first chakra is the expression of pure, natural, cosmic energy. The second is cell division and the development of all organic life, in all its forms. The third is the development of society and settlements, the beginning of culture and civilization. The fourth was marked by the appearance of Christ and the new idea of joining the divine consciousness and existence through man, emphasizing divine love as the principle of consciousness and existence. The fifth chakra represents the uniting of the world and people on an information level - the start of education and literacy, the beginning and development of critical thinking. It denotes the period from the Renaissance to modern day living. The sixth chakra will be the correct perception of objective reality and its implementation in this world. That is yet to come, due in the following centuries. It will be the age of the quantum mind, and will bring together all of the ancient knowledge of the divine consciousness with the subatomic world, the practical realization of quantum consciousness and an awareness of the essence of nature. Once this has been properly implemented, only then will the seventh chakra be fully realized, as the presence of the divine consciousness in this world through man and their deeds. This can happen only in the next millennium.

The principles of chakra functioning in the world can be observed through the manner of living. The lower chakras are a characteristic of natural existence, that apart from its beauty and vitality contain all unconsciousness and baseness. Everything that is ugly, bad, restricting and unworthy of man is a characteristic of the manifestation of the lower centers. Everything that is exalted, beautiful and harmonious, the obvious result of work and knowledge, perfection, liberation and creation is a characteristic of the manifestation of the higher centers. All of this is inseparable from human actions and the state of consciousness. That is why the principles of functioning in the world are the same as in man, and why there is the system of chakras: the state of the world cannot be divided from the state and deeds of man. **The system of chakras unites the outer world with human psyche and actions.** In other words, a human's reality is not separated from the reality of the world they live in. If this does happen, it is due to dysfunctionality in the operating of the centers, and insufficient consciousness in man.

The more consciousness is realized through the upper chakras, the bigger the influence of consciousness and understanding of everything lower; the more consciousness is tied in its functioning to the lower chakras, the more it is restricted, disintegrated and divided. This is how it is reflected in the world.

The evolution of consciousness on this planet, through material culture and the development of civilization, is conducted only through the activation of the consciousness through the higher chakras.

EXAMPLES OF CHAKRA FUNCTIONING IN THE HISTORY OF SPIRITUALITY

The Hertzian nature of chakras and their polarization are the key component to all true spirituality, although phrasing may vary through time. Perhaps the best example of this is the teaching of the Buddhist reformer from the second century, Nagarjuna, who established the two aspects of reality: the absolute (*paramartha*) or transcendent one (non-Hertzian), and the relative (*samvrti*) or empirical one (Hertzian). The absolute one refers to the nature of ether or the quantum field, which in simple words can be described as emptiness (*sunya*). Today, we refer to it as the awareness of now. Nagarjuna taught that although we empirically experience only the manifested, Hertzian aspect of existence, it essentially still resides in the non-Hertzian aspect, in ether or the quantum consciousness. It could not exist otherwise, because the very nature of the quantum field has no plural. Therefore, nothing exists all by itself. He taught that the void of the quantum field is at the heart of all matter and phenomena, and that our final cognition or state of awareness is one and the same quantum consciousness.

Lao Tzu also spoke of this when he pointed to the difference between Tao (the non-Hertzian aspect) and Te (the Hertzian aspect), and when he condensed all our wisdom to the ability to distinguish between the two aspects of reality in the nature of existence, as well as in any action we undertake.

The science of tantra, from pre-Vedic India to the Chinese alchemists, works with these two aspects of consciousness; all energy emanates from the psychoenergetic centers or chakras.

The essence of Patanjali's practice of yoga, or meditation, consists of the idea of achieving pure transcendental consciousness, which is exactly the type of consciousness that expresses itself through the quantum field. Meditation or mental stillness is found by achieving a non-Hertzian state of mind, and such a mind resonates in harmony with the universal quantum field.

In the works of Carlos Castaneda, the Hertzian frequency of existence is described as *tonal*, and the non-Hertzian as *nagual*.

In other spiritual traditions this reality is hidden away, made into myth or dogma. Only the recent discoveries in quantum physics revealed the connection between the nature of the quantum field and ancient teachings.[12]

---

[12] See more on this in the Fritjof Capra book: *The Tao Of Physics*.

EXAMPLES OF CHAKRA FUNCTIONING IN THE PERSONAL DEVELOPMENT OF HUMANS

In human development there is a process of energy exchange in which we can recognize the impact of the chakras. For example, the second chakra is in charge of sexuality; more precisely, it is in charge of the exchange of energy with the opposite sex. If expressed without a higher consciousness, without the consciousness of the higher third chakra, it will remain tied to the lower, first chakra, and then such sexuality will be manifested as a raw energy exchange, usually expressed in a promiscuous way. The influence of the second chakra refers to any kind of partying or hedonism. If sexual energy exchange becomes connected with the awareness of the higher, third chakra, it will express itself as a permanent union of a loving couple planning a family. This is quite a bit more meaningful than the temporary satisfaction of mere sexual exchange. Actually, only with such a connection with the consciousness of the higher chakra can sexual exchange be considered a true exchange that brings forth genuine pleasure. If it is aimed at itself only, it causes a loss of energy. Every chakra reaches its true potential only when it is directed at the values of the next higher chakra.

Practically, this means that sex without love upsets the energy balance. For this reason, it continually seeks balance and fulfillment, but always in the wrong way, by changing partners; that is, by repeating the same mistake of connecting consciousness of the second chakra to the first, rather than the third chakra. To direct consciousness from the second to the higher, third chakra, one should understand that sex is not merely for fun, but for conception, and for love; it is the most intimate and the most beautiful expression of love.

When the requirements of the third chakra have been met, meaning there is a permanent union of two people and offspring is the higher goal of life energy, then we are met with the functioning of the fourth chakra, the act of love. Then energy is exchanged with all of existence, and not just the opposite sex. Once we are acquainted with life and see it develop through the child we brought into this world, we are forced to recognize that life and consciousness exists in all children, in all beings, and throughout all of existence. This is how the fourth chakra, anahata, becomes activated. When it is active, unconditional divine love is recognized throughout existence. Maybe we conceived a child for reasons of love (the transition from the second to the third chakra), but this child, once we get to know it, reveals the presence of divine love, which the realization of the fourth chakra brings us. Children are born out of love, and only out of love. Only children filled with love can implement all these processes correctly.

The full activation of the higher chakras, the fifth, sixth and seventh, in the higher intellectual center, is a matter of individual growth and conscious effort, and spiritual work on oneself; their full potential is realized by just a tiny few, although it is out there for everyone, available for the taking. If there is a hindrance, it is only ignorance and malfunctioning of the lower enters. Hence, the fifth chakra indicates the ability to communicate based on all previously acquired maturity, as a result of the growth of consciousness through the lower chakras. All the words of wise men that have stood the test of time come from this chakra. The sixth chakra is the ability to view all things clearly. The seventh chakra is pure consciousness of oneself.

Although the topic here is the gradual activation of chakras, what we have in mind is their full activation and realization of their potential. They all, however, already function in their most basic form. The first chakra gives us all our life energy; the second gives us all sensual joys, fun and pleasure; the third enables awareness of some joint goal - every time we do something with other people, when we work on benefiting the community, we use the potential of the third chakra; the fourth, heart chakra we use with every manifestation of emotional maturity, of love and compassion, and true understanding and unity with the whole; in the fifth chakra we speak and express our maturity; in the sixth we perceive everything that can be perceived, even what goes beyond standard sensory perception. In the seventh chakra we are connected with the consciousness of our soul, and with the divine consciousness that enables everything. From it we receive consciousness into all the other chakras. Every chakra is realized by strengthening of the consciousness of itself. With the proper functioning of chakras, awareness turns back to itself, to sahasrara, to samadhi, to the unity of consciousness and existence.

Whenever we do something positive and right, we sublimate the consciousness from the lower to the higher chakras. When we do something negative and destructive, we lower our consciousness to the lower centers.

Through a normal individual, life energy flows and ascends in the stated order; this is how chakras are activated and the way man grows. Everything that is not normal in man and human society takes place when this growth is stopped or blocked in the first three centers, or when the functioning of the energy centers becomes mixed somehow, or disrupted altogether. We can see that, in the end, divine consciousness merges in the highest chakra with itself, through an awakened individual, in samadhi. The divine consciousness as unconditional love is the strongest force in all existence. It incites everything, and it has the strongest pull. Everything revolves around it. It is accessible to every man through the fourth, heart chakra, through the experience of love.

In order for this psychoenergetic development to be properly finalized, it is necessary for man at the very beginning of their life to go through the experience of unconditional divine love; first to have an idea of what it really is, and that it can exist in this world, because many adversities can keep it in hiding. This divine, unconditional, absolute love and kindness a child can and must experience through parental love and motherly hug and gentleness. That is all that's required, for the rest of a human's lifetime, so that they know it exists and it is possible, and so they can correctly develop through all their energy centers, and to be able to transfer this experience to another individual. Those who never experienced it in childhood and do not know or believe that it exists, that unconditional love and goodness are possible in this world, will attempt to seek it elsewhere, throughout their lives, including through deviant means, since those are the greatest attractions and motivation.

All of human creation rests on this aspiration. All of the evil among people is brought about in the same way: due to a lack of experience of love and goodness, due to a lack of belief that they are possible. (It is not in vain when we hear a violent person explained with "his mother did not love him". Very often, this is the true cause of their antisocial behavior.) All positive human deeds testify to the various aspects of experiencing divine consciousness, love and goodness, and all wrongdoings testify to the lack of this experience.

Two additional matters need to be mentioned here. Firstly, in ancient societies, in the original human communities of this world, there was a tradition which naturally conducted consciousness in every individual from the lower to the higher chakras. All customs and norms were actually made for this purpose.

The term dharma in Indian tradition connects the cosmic order with human life and development. The second crucial fact that should be known about the functioning of the chakras, especially their dysfunctional operating, is that the rulers of this world, who generate all the negativity on this planet, as well as material progress, focus their attention on disrupting the proper functioning of the chakras - particularly the first three, including sexuality; most commonly they display all the perversions and unconscious licentiousness of the lower centers and depict them as 'human rights and freedoms'.

By doing so, they pervert true human rights and freedoms. They're actually only do their job - they cause states opposite to normal ones, so they misdirect consciousness to the lower centers instead of the higher centers. They keep doing this to force a man to use the impact of their personal experience of everything wrong to reach awareness of what is actually right. In the laws of this world (the category of dialectics – the unity of opposites) this is the only way for consciousness to manifest itself fully. Consciousness is unable to manifest itself if instigated by an outer source, outside our being. Consciousness can manifest and actualize itself only with the assistance of consciousness itself, and there can be no consciousness without the experience of existence. Such is the nature of consciousness.

THE ENERGETIC CHAKRA ACTIVATION

Since the connection of consciousness with existence is expressed as life energy, *prana*, and also the strength we put into our every effort and endeavor, the movement of consciousness between levels of existence, meaning chakras, is simultaneously experienced as an energetic phenomenon. A sudden movement of this energy along the chakras is felt as a thrill, full of rapture, which overtakes us and lifts upward through the spine, anytime we experience a revelation, or when we do something good, beautiful and important. The state of energy also affects the state of consciousness.

Every conscious sublimation into higher understanding and more creative functioning is followed by a rise in energy. Such greater connection of consciousness and energy is called 'positive energy'. The more aware we are while using our energy, the more positive it becomes. Every decline of consciousness into the lower and conditioned states is usually followed by a loss and sapping of life energy. It is experienced as negative energy'. This is always followed by blackouts. The basic characteristic of positive energy is the surpassing of mechanical conditioning; it spreads out, away from itself, because the essence of consciousness is the power to recognize that all is joined as one. The basic characteristic of negative energy is isolation from the whole, a need to take energy away from other beings or to exchange it by force, due to a lack of consciousness of the unity of existence, and the omnipresence of energy and consciousness.

The nature of energy in the lower chakras is more Hertzian in its properties. This means that it is more polarized, linear, and more suited for the three-dimensional world. This reflects on the psyche, and makes it even more polarized, and hence more divided into opposites, and in conflict with itself and the outside world.

This polarization creates even greater tension.

Greater tension gives the individual mind (ego) a greater illusion of power, importance and significance. Therefore, when the mind is exposed to a larger energy polarization, it interprets it as greater vitality and greater reality. That is partly why the lower chakras have such a strong attraction. With their own energy polarization they give the illusion that they are more important and more real; this creates more identification for a feeble consciousness, so consciousness identifies easier with this reality, full of conflicts and passion. People find it hard to rise above their habits and passions. The power of attraction of the lowest psychoenergetic centers, which are polarized to the maximum, is the cause of all reincarnations, and the fall of man into the lower states of consciousness, and all suffering. All dualism in man has its source here; they are chained to their lower nature, to illusions of material existence, while at the same time he can be aware of consciousness itself and its independence of everything. He refers to it as their lower and their higher nature.

The energetic chakra rising is easiest to comprehend through the nature of their frequencies. The first chakra, muladhara, is maximally Hertzian, while the last chakra, sahasrara, is maximally non-Hertzian. This is why the first is maximally polarized into opposites and expresses its nature most obviously as pure energy, its impact being material to the greatest extent. The seventh chakra is, for the same reason, the most distanced from materiality and closest to the unity of opposites. All the remaining chakras merely represent stages of manifestation, all the way from pure energy to pure consciousness. All the chakras together represent the unity of energy and consciousness; that is, the manifested existence in consciousness and in all possible phases, from the Hertzian to the non-Hertzian.

In practical experience, this means that the first chakra provides pure life energy; more accurately, the energy wholeness of our being. It is best observed in a young being who is so energetically whole that it has the power of regeneration. The second chakra functions in such a manner that the original energy wholeness begins to divide and polarize - expressed as sexuality. From that moment onward the energy wholeness is achieved and restored through direct intercourse with the energy of the opposite sex, or polarity. It is also a necessary condition for creating a new life (conception).

In the act of unity, ecstasy appears for a moment and provides the experience of the original unity of consciousness and existence, through orgasm. In the third chakra, energy is exchanged with the wider community, who are not connected via a biological relationship; This is like in the second chakra, but it is extended to all the life interests that people share. In this ever widening concept of sharing and relationships, the energy reaches the point of wholeness. In the fourth chakra, the energy exchange is maximally widespread and versatile; it refers to all objects and forms of existence, without any differences or limitations in its relationships and contents.

For the first time, the Hertzian frequencies of energy manifestation (the first, three lower chakras) lose dominance and are equalized with, or transformed into, the non-Hertzian ones; more precisely, the physical and energetic experience of existence transforms into the spiritual and conscious (the three upper chakras). We experience this awareness of the energetic unity of everything as the feeling of love. In the central chakra, anahata, a precise measuring and weighing of the manifested and the unmanifested takes place, a weighing of the material and conscious, of the spiritual, the outer and the inner. This measuring and balancing through the energetic experience of comprehending everything is emotional maturity; in other words, one's ability to love. Love becomes the prerequisite for the proper understanding of everything, a condition for every type of awareness. In the end, the final awakening will find its balance in the proper functioning of this chakra.

The next form of existence, with the aim of energetic wholeness, refers to the exchange of experience and information. That is the fifth chakra, vishuddhi. The next is complete cognition and perception of energy as a form of consciousness, and takes place in the sixth chakra, ajna. Energy and consciousness finally marry here; that is, energy, every form of existence, is recognized as consciousness, and consciousness is recognized as every possible form of life. Once this is realized, the transcendence of form and consciousness in the seventh chakra, sahasrara, immediately occurs.

In this way, existence through all chakras travels through the rough physical or the Hertzian state to the more subtle nonphysical or non-Hertzian state. Following this pattern, those two states, from their ostensible opposition – which gives the illusion of the manifested world – become one state of divine consciousness, the soul's consciousness.

In order for the energy aspect of chakras to be harmonized, allowing for its sublimation, it is necessary to work with chakras from two aspects: the energetic and the psychological - that is, consciously.

In the system of practice of G. I. Gurdjieff, the relationship between energy and consciousness is expressed in the terms 'work on the being' which refers to energy, and 'work on the knowledge' which refers to consciousness. It is very important that both of these are well-balanced and even. The work on the being consists of a series of small exercises which sublimate the energy potential of the body. It affects the state of mind. Unless this work is followed by work on acquiring knowledge, which brings an understanding of the entire process - that is, objective awareness and an understanding of what energy really is, what goals it should have and its effect on consciousness - then their balance is off, and it misdirects human development. Likewise, if work on acquiring knowledge is not followed by work on being, the accumulation and correct implementation of energy, then such consciousness will be of no use to anyone; it will remain abstract. It will not possess sufficient energy to realize its true potential.

The energy work with chakras consists of the right diet and certain exercises.

The conscious work with chakras entails strengthening the presence of awareness, and understanding the functioning and effect it has on all states of consciousness, in all the chakras. That is the practice of meditation.

A good diet is the foundation for the proper operating of all the chakras, especially of the lower three. They are more dependent on the quality of energy, and energy is taken in largely through food. Raw plant food is ideal for the well-balanced functioning of the lower centers.

Rougher food (cooked, non-vegetarian) strengthens the functioning of these chakras, and they are harder to overcome. Due to the lack of consciousness and an excess of energy, the functioning of the lower chakras is easier to disturb.

There are multiple exercises for 'sublimating the energy' through the chakras; *hatha yoga* is focused on this, and a great deal of tantra practice; they involve imagination (*yantra*) and sound vibration (*mantra*) in connection with every single chakra.

However, the majority of these exercises are ideologically oriented. For this reason, we do not deal with them, because we only put forward the objective reality in connection with chakras, respectively the unity of consciousness and existence.

We will suggest only two exercises here that are completely effective and ideologically neutral.

The first is known as the *Tibetan Rejuvenation Rites Program*; exercises which were gathered and published by Peter Kelder in the work *Ancient Secret of the Fountain of Youth*.

The second exercise is the 'circulation of light,' taken from the book *The Secret of the Golden Flower,* a manual in Tao alchemy translated by Richard Wilhelm, which will be presented here in somewhat altered form, influenced by the experiences published in *Kundalini Tantra* by Swami Satyananda Saraswati.

These books should be studied for better understanding of this topic.

PHYSICAL EXERCISES FOR HARMONIOUS CHAKRA ACTIVATION

These exercises have been taken from Peter Kelder's book *The Fountain of Youth*, and are universal and easy for every healthy individual, with the goal of harmonious chakra activation and to maintain overall health and vitality.

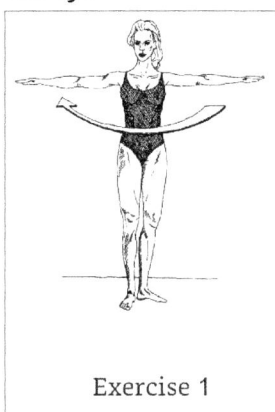

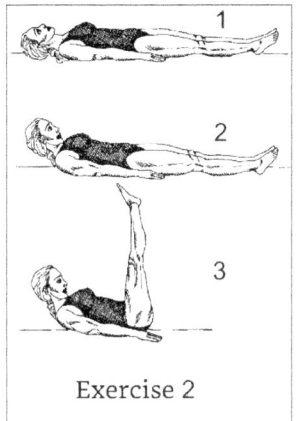

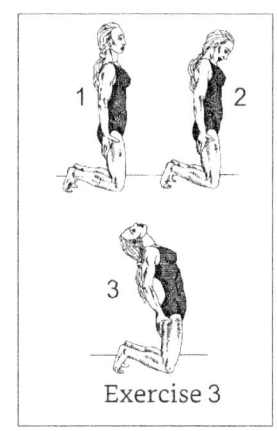

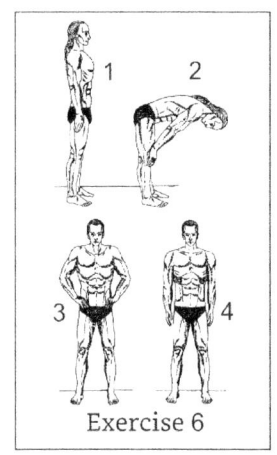

Exercise 1

Exercise 2

Exercise 3

Exercise 4

Exercise 5

Exercise 6

The first five exercises, or rites, are done together, one after another. The sixth is done separately.

Breathing in the first five exercises is done through the nose, every time we bend backward or lift the body, and breathing out is done through the mouth, when we put down the legs or the body.

The first five exercises activate all the chakras, and sublimate energy in the body. They are done on a daily basis, every morning and evening, with a twelve-hour time span. Beginners should start with three repetitions of each exercise, and gradually increase the performance to an odd number only, until they reach twenty-one. From that moment onward, they do all the elements 21 times in total, ideally for the rest of one's life. The first exercise is performed by spinning round, till we reach 21 turns.

The sixth exercise serves to lift energy (specifically sexual energy) accumulated in the lower chakras upward to the higher chakras. This exercise is done only when we have excess sexual energy and we wish to redirect it. The first five exercises greatly enhance the energy potential in the body, together with sexual energy, which is proof that these exercises work. If there is no excess sexual energy, this exercise is of no use. It is also of no use if the person is not mature enough to redirect sexual energy from the lower to the higher chakras. It should also be stressed that the first five exercises are incomplete without the sixth.

The sixth exercise consists of breathing only. In the body position shown under number 1 we exhale through the mouth all the air from the lungs, and at the same time bend until we get to position 2, with empty lungs. Then, with empty lungs, return to an upright posture as shown in 3. Put your hands on your hips, and so we stay as long as possible with empty lungs. When we can no longer stand, we just let our hands go as in figure 4 and let the air flow into the lungs through the nose. Breathe evenly a few times, until breathing returns to normal. This exercise should be repeated several times.

This exercise is a powerful tool for the transformation of sexual energy to the higher centers. It acts as a vacuum pump, and instantly releases unnecessary sexual tension. With its simplicity, the futile attempts made by monks and 'spiritual' people to restrain their sexual energy seem comical, done often to suppress sexuality; a practice that later backfires in many deviant ways, often pseudo religious. Actually, the majority of pseudo religiousness is spiked with the poison of suppressed sexuality.

The energy is always one and the same. The same energy generates sexuality and the mind. It is only a question of what level of consciousness (chakra) it operates from. One would do well to get acquainted with it first, to get to know its ways of functioning, and afterward to redirect it to the higher centers.

Without getting to know it and fully comprehending the way it functions, it is not possible to redirect energy from the lower to the higher centers. Comprehending itself is in essence what redirects and improves function, and expression. Comprehension is awareness, and energy always follows awareness, like the shadow of a traveler follows the light.

THE EXERCISE OF IMAGINATION AND BREATHING FOR CHAKRA ACTIVATION

Apart from these exercises for work with chakras, only one additional exercise is required.

Firstly, one should become aware of the positions of all seven chakras in the body, and their colors. After that, with the inhaling of air through the nose, one should visualize white light in the form of a stream that moves in an upward direction from the first chakra onto the second, as though the inhaling itself lifts and sucks in the light energy; then one should exhale through the mouth. As one breathes for the second time, visualize the white stream of light energy lifting from the second chakra to the third. Exhale. Then do the same from the third to the fourth, from the fourth to the fifth, from the fifth to the sixth, and finally from the sixth to the seventh.

With every inhale we take, we lift the light stream of energy one chakra higher. Once we reach the seventh chakra, we exhale slowly, and visualize the white light cascading down like a shower, around the whole body, from the seventh chakra down to the first, where it gathers again; and then we repeat the cycle of seven inhalations and seven exhalations of the white energy stream, from one chakra to another. This can be called the circulation of light. We finish after a third repetition; and the final cycle we complete by lowering the light, not to the first chakra as before, but only to the heart. So, the whole exercise is done three times, after which the light energy is settled in the heart.

This can be done after the previously described exercises for chakra activation, or it can be done totally independent of them, whenever possible, at a minimum once a day.

THE PRINCIPLE OF ENERGY PRESERVATION
FOR THE SUBLIMATION OF CONSCIOUSNESS

The most important factor in raising awareness of all chakras and attaining samadhi is the preservation of energy in the body. This is because energy is the physical reflection of consciousness, what the consciousness does in existence; energy is the power of the consciousness to act in the body and in existence, and consciousness is intention or purpose the energy acts in accordance with. Therefore, energy and consciousness are two aspects of the same thing, one somewhat rougher and one more subtle.

To strengthen the presence of consciousness in the body, it is necessary to strengthen the presence of energy. In other words: *it is necessary to preserve the energy from the first chakra in all other chakras; that is, in the various methods of existence and states of consciousness.* It is necessary because, when every chakra functions with its full energy potential, then consciousness through every chakra realizes its full potential.

The most basic form of energy exchange in the body is with sexual energy. The carriers of that energy are sexual cells. Therefore, in order to preserve the body's energy as much as possible, it is necessary to preserve these sexual cells. The sexual cells are created through the joint effort of all the glands in the endocrine system. All chakras participate in their creation. This is why, whenever we lose sexual cells through sexuality that does not have the purpose of creating a new life, we lose potential from all of the chakras. It is of key importance that we preserve sexual cells, to be able to sublimate the consciousness to the highest chakra. When they are not secreted, but remain in the body, sexual cells are absorbed by the blood, and then enhance the performance of neurotransmitters in the brain, thus boosting perception. People who abstain from sex know that they have better memory, concentration, and even sometimes extrasensory perception.

All it takes is for energy to be preserved, by preserving the sexual cells in the body. Then the energy will naturally ascend from the lower to the higher centers, all the way to the seventh chakra. This resembles filling up a jar with water, all the way to the top. If there is a tiny hole at the bottom of a jar, we can never fill it. In a similar fashion, one should prevent energy from being sapped through the lower chakras, in order to fill to the top. We lose energy through the malfunctioning of centers, and through negativity. More accurately, negativity is the obvious outcome of malfunctioning psychoenergetic centers. Preventing energy from draining away is possible only with the proper functioning of the lower chakras - by getting fully and consciously acquainted with the way they operate and an understanding of the process. Further help may be found in the previously explained exercises.

The preservation of sexual cells, sexual energy, and its redirection to the higher centers, a.k.a. the science of tantra, is the primary goal in the practice of awakening or enlightenment. To avoid the dangerous and harmful suppression of sexual energy, tantra teaches us to raise awareness of sexuality itself, through intercourse, but without ejaculation and orgasmic energy discharge. By doing so, the entire act transfers energy upward into the higher, heart chakra, anahata; the sex itself is surpassed and real love making is experienced. The fourth heart chakra is the cognition of the energetic essence of existence, and when consciousness and energy combine, it is experienced as love making, since energy binds everything and love always strives to be in unity with the loved one.

One should make love with the purpose of experiencing the other being in the most profound way, and not for the sake of one's own desires. You make love with touch and sight, but above all through mutual understanding, common feelings and joint cognition - with your whole existence, not just with one body; with the whole being, in all aspects of life, and not just the sexual organs. That is why love always gives, and asks nothing in return. Making love means enjoying the soul's consciousness together with another soul - enjoying, together, the consciousness of existence. The result of such love making is not a sudden and short-lived discharge, ecstasy-like in normal intercourse, but a permanent ecstasy rooted in the deepest fulfillment, with the knowledge, understanding and clarity that means love. And energy. If we preserve the sexual cells that propagate new life, they will fertilize us, they will fill us with the perpetual bliss, and with a permanent orgasm. And this will rejuvenate our body.

The experience of orgasm is nothing but a short-lived experience of the bliss found in the complete merging of consciousness and existence, samadhi. That is why orgasms are so appealing. If we preserve our energy, we will remain in such a state forever.

Actually, the proper functioning of every chakra, and all the chakras together, does not depend on anything but the balance of energy and consciousness in each chakra. This means that it depends on the balance and unity of our thoughts and deeds, consciousness and will, knowledge and work. This is why chakras exist in the first place: to link consciousness and existence through our being.

The connection of energy and consciousness is clear thanks to the very nature of energy and consciousness. Energy means a being in movement and action, and consciousness always expresses itself as being, as existence. Therefore, one without the other is not possible.

Our body is a microcosm. Everything in the cosmos is compressed in the body as well. Energy is everything that takes place in the cosmos, and everything that could be; therefore, energy is the compressed event of everything that can possibly happen. We have already stated that thought is information for further shaping, that thought and shape co-exist in parallel, and that they are one and the same thing even though they appear to be separate due to the different dimensions of reality they occupy; so on the outside we have a form, and within us we have the thought of the form. The same works for energy and every event: the energy is the finest expression of an event, it is the potential (information) for any possible future outcome, and no event can ever take place without energy. *What happens in the outside world also happens within us, in the form of pure energy*. What information is to shaping, energy is to happening. Energy is the most subtle form of happening, information for events.

All events find their endpoint in consciousness, in the knowing of the sense of an event. Therefore, in order for us to reach the highest consciousness, to the endpoint of all happening, we must experience any potential event within us first, as the microcosm; we must beat all the temptations of the lower chakras, all the lower states of consciousness and happening. We achieve this by keeping and condensing within ourselves the potential of all possible events, in their original informational form, as energy to preserve and compress within ourselves. This is how we raise awareness of the happening within ourselves. This is the true meaning of preserving and sublimating energy along the chakras for the sake of consciousness. By preserving energy within us, we keep all the possibilities in their most original, informational form. Therefore, the more energy we have, the more awareness we possess. To be the most aware we must contain all the potential of being and existence (energy) in ourselves. If we do not have energy, we do not hold potential of all possible events in ourselves, in our body, and therefore have nothing to raise awareness of. This is why consciousness is always present wherever there is energy.

We must never project awareness onto the outside. Everything is resolved within us. Due to the omnipresent energy, the uniting of consciousness and existence through the chakras, only what we become aware of in our own system, what we comprehend, overcome and surpass within ourselves, will we be able to raise awareness of, comprehend, overcome and surpass in the outside world. It never goes the other way. Existence does not reach awareness of itself, of the meaning of phenomena, through objects or animals, but instead through the creation of our bodies and the chakra system; this is the most suitable place for it to reach final awareness of itself. That is why in our bodies, all the potential of our existence – energy – has to exist, in order for all the potential of consciousness to be expressed. This is why they are both in the final outcome, one and the same.

THE BASIC PRINCIPLES OF SUBLIMATING CONSCIOUSNESS THROUGH CHAKRAS

Consciousness as the source of existence is present everywhere, in all chakras; chakras exist as psycho-energy centers to enable the actualization of consciousness in a specific way. The method of actualization or functioning of consciousness in the world, or being, corresponds to the functioning of a certain chakra. Therefore, the presence of consciousness in a certain chakra relates to the manner in which we exist and act. All we have to do is to actualize the consciousness, not to bring it into a certain chakra. It is already present, as the very foundation of life; the only question that remains is what to do with it.

Therefore, when we say that we should activate a certain chakra, what is usually meant is that we should act in accordance with the level of consciousness corresponding with the characteristics of that chakra.

Every higher chakra is activated by raising awareness of the functioning of the lower chakra.

In order for consciousness to be taken to higher levels, nothing much should be done besides harmonizing the functioning of every single chakra to do the job it was designed to do, and not to meddle with the functioning of the others, so that the functioning of the psycho-energy centers remains unperturbed. All the drama of human life and all adversity can be reduced to mere disruption in the functioning of the chakras, and nothing more.

Here is a simple example of the malfunctioning of the centers. If the functioning of the second chakra, sexuality, is disrupted by the functioning of the third chakra, which means expressing your will, (and when imagination from the higher centers is added), and this is combined with the strength of the first chakra, which adds the power of raw energy, then the result is deviant sexual conduct, or a mind burdened with inferior behavior, with sexuality and materialism. The functioning of every chakra is correct only when it is restricted to its function in accordance with its own level. Sexuality is right only when it serves its purpose, but when it is mixed with the other centers it disrupts the functioning of both sexuality and other centers. There is nothing wrong with the functioning of any specific chakra. The problem is when their functioning is disrupted and when they do not perform the task they were originally designed to perform.

In every single chakra there are two parts, one lower and one higher: the mechanical and the conscious; our task is to enhance the presence of consciousness in the conscious part, which is done by awakening the mechanical functioning of that specific chakra.

Therefore, everything can be boiled down to awakening and understanding. This is the sole route to higher states of existence. Consequently, awakening and understanding that is in harmony with our functioning (energy) is all that's required. This bond is necessary, because neither correct functioning is possible without consciousness, nor is proper consciousness of existence possible without proper conduct. Let us remind ourselves here that energy means action.

However, when we speak of consciousness, we primarily refer to its quantum field and the non-Hertzian nature of existence. Practically this means that while sublimating consciousness and energy into the higher chakras, the non-Hertzian properties should be enhanced.

These properties include: a timeless presence, here and now, that is a consequence of the independence of consciousness from the contents of the mind; a state of infinite present, as the only reality - there is nothing that needs to take place in the future, everything is already realized in the here and now; a feeling that we do not move around in space but that space moves around us - there is not a significant difference between what is without and what is within, the outside world is merely a reflection of the consciousness within us, and synchronicity points out and proves this in the form of the merging of consciousness and phenomena. Therefore, the non-Hertzian state of consciousness connects us to the universal quantum field, where everything is ever present in a timeless and subtle way, including the fullest potential of every single chakra.

The Hertzian properties belong to the mechanical functioning of each chakra, as well as to the mechanical and conditional functioning in general. Above all, linear time and causality is based on it. The non-Hertzian properties of each chakra belongs to the consciousness and conscious functioning, independent and free, and always omnipresent.

The practice of meditation is the only practice that strengthens non-Hertzian consciousness of the quantum field.

When we refer to the idea of meditation, what we actually mean is the pure practice of transcendence of the mind (mental stillness), which is a part of the practice of early Buddhism (*dhyana*), in zen Buddhism (*za zen*, *shikan taza*), described in the opening chapters of the *Yoga Sutras* by Patanjali.

The basic non-Hertzian property of the quantum field is staticity and self-sufficiency. On our physical plane, it is stillness of the being which produces the feeling of perfect completion and realization, the bliss of finding oneself and one's own essence. When our being is completely still, when we sit through the meditative process, moving from rough physical motion to the finest mental stillness, we adjust ourselves to the stationary, non-Hertzian, universal quantum field. This is why meditation is the direct path to the non-Hertzian, quantum consciousness, which is the very source of existence.

The strengthening of the non-Hertzian state of consciousness refers as much to mental stillness as it does to energetic adjusting. Because energy is a being in motion and action, consciousness is in motion and action. Hence, there is nothing we can do with consciousness unless it is followed by energy and action. We must bring energy into a non-Hertzian state. We do this by understanding the nature of our actions on the energy level, what we do and why, with conscious awareness of our actions. By raising awareness of every movement of our being, from breathing consciously to the smallest movement we make, we bring our energy in harmony with consciousness - we become aware of it, and by doing so we translate it to the non-Hertzian state. In Buddhism this practice is called *vipassana* and *satipatthana*.

Such awareness is systematically being conducted in all the dimensions of our existence: in the physical body (earth), in feelings and emotions (water); by expressing will and intention (fire); and becoming aware of the mind itself (air). Only such a practice can connect all the states of consciousness into the seventh condition, the seventh chakra *sahasrara*, into samadhi, into the unity of consciousness and existence.

All of this is possible only because this unity is already in existence, and everything else builds on this existence. Everything we do in this world and in all our lives is to rediscover this unity. The divine consciousness is the only reality, and nothing can exist outside of it. We can merely manifest it, completely and individually in samadhi, in us and through us; in samadhi we unite the divine consciousness that enables everything, with itself, in itself, by uniting our individual consciousness with the divine consciousness.

If they were not already in unity, their ostensible unity could never occur to us.

To make this happen man need just strengthen their non-Hertzian state of consciousness, their timeless presence in the here and now. The energy of the quantum field will be able to manifest itself through such an awakened individual, giving him/her a limitless supply of the omnipresent energy based on the non-Hertzian waves.

What is the practical aspect of consciousness and energy being sublimated through the chakras? That is the key question of those who practice spirituality. The answer is simple, and we have already given it: every higher chakra is activated by raising the awareness of the lower chakra.

This process has a natural tendency to realize itself fully, and if it does not do so it is due to our mind/ego disrupting the whole system. These disruptions take place continually. All our lives are based on these disruptions. Consciousness tests all possibilities, which means all mistakes as well. If the uniting of existence and consciousness were happening along a straight line, with no faltering and no decline, consciousness would be unable to integrate itself with all the aspects and possibilities of existence - there would be nothing to become aware of. It is the very oscillations, the rising and falling, that give the necessary friction that charges the energy and makes it express itself in an endless variety of ways, making consciousness strengthen its presence in all states of being and existence. This is the only way for it to grow in the upward manner along the chakras.

Come what may, chakras are already doing their job. Our task is simply to be aware of their performance in our minds, and by doing so to actualize it in our existence. Therefore, it can be said that chakra activation is actually about making the mind aware of their functioning. Once this happens, the functioning of the chakras will embrace our whole being, both the conscious and the unconscious part.

How does this awareness of chakra functioning look to our experience? All chakras work together, and it is hard in life to tell their functioning apart, although there are general rules of thumb for each chakra. All chakras are in an interconnected chain of functioning. This chain has a positive impact, and chakras express themselves properly only if the lower one is tied in its functioning to the higher one. If a chakra is closed off and limited to its functions only, or perhaps tied to the lower chakra, then its functioning is negative.

***

The first chakra gives life energy to the whole body and all the other chakras. As such it is neutral. It is successfully realized through the second chakra, where energy is polarized, and this polarization is expressed through sexuality. More accurately, the polarized energy must be exchanged - it must circulate through man and woman. For this reason, human beings exist as two sexes. Sex is nothing but the exchange of energy between the two sexes. Through sex new life is born, and our energy status very much depends on what we do with our energy through sexuality. When the first chakra is successfully expressed through the second chakra, life energy (the energy of the first chakra) successfully expresses itself through all the activities connected with simple energy exchange through physical contact - with all objects, with the opposite sex, with other beings and in various situations (fun, games, all kinds of physical contact and relationships, and aggressiveness within the normal boundaries). With the correct exchange of energy, and its adequate polarization, our body is healthy and vital.

Without a real connection to the higher chakras, life energy from the first chakra becomes the opposition to life; such men must take life energy by force from other beings, and he does so in a number of twisted ways. All abnormal ways of taking life energy, from murder to abuse and energy vampirism in any form, are the direct result of the first energy block and the lack of any real connection with the higher centers and soul's consciousness.

***

The second chakra is properly actualized through the third chakra, when we focus energy on a higher goal and purpose, during the exchange of energy with another being or community, and focus on the joint interests of the community we share time and space with. If we exchange our energy with the opposite sex and aim for some higher purpose, such as offspring or the realization of some higher goals and ideals, then we have successfully activated the third chakra. The nature of one chakra reaches its full potential only when it is dedicated to a higher psycho-energy center. This is true for sexuality also; it is the source of the greatest joy only if it is aimed at a higher purpose, if it does not serve itself only, and as long as it is not aimed at a lower center. Then it becomes destructive. One form of destructiveness is when the energy in the second chakra is not exchanged with the opposite sex, but is with the same sex (or worse yet, with something else). Then the circulation of energy between the sexes does not take place, and neither does the healing which takes the energy to the higher centers; but instead it is blocked in the second chakra. Homosexuality is energetically wrong, it is just blocking off energy in the second chakra.

When the first three chakras are successfully connected and activated they conduct the energy in a positive way, within every man and in interpersonal relationships. When sexuality is good, the flow of energy from the first to the third chakra is good. Disturbance of sexuality (second chakra) is largely the cause of other disturbances (the first chakra: psychophysical health; and third chakra: social life and life goals).

Without the real connection between the second chakra and the third, energy in the second chakra remains locked and self-sufficient, in its most basic form, so it becomes destructive; due to the lack of higher consciousness, the second chakra can find its energy exchange with all sorts of things, not just with the opposite sex of the same biological species. Energy exchange can happen with any object. This is how all perversions and obsessions (fetishism) are brought about, and consequently all unhealthy interpersonal relationships.

***

In order to successfully actualize the third chakra we should connect it with the fourth chakra. The fourth means understanding that our basic goals and aspirations rest on love and understanding. The fourth chakra is a consciousness of the omnipresent energy; it does not refer only to our body (the first two chakras) nor the environment and society (third chakra), but to existence in general. The awareness that we are one with existence is love. This is why we can love everything: a certain being or a certain thing, place, music, book, plant, animal... even what is not healthy to love.

In order to realize the third chakra successfully, for example through children and family, the fourth chakra must also be realized, as the third cannot fully exist without omnipresent love and emotional maturity. The realization of the third chakra, the fulfillment of a life goal, or the birth of a child, connects us to the omnipresent energy, to all of existence, through the fourth chakra. Namely, when we have become completely aware of what it was that we are striving for through the third chakra (for example the birth of a child), we recognize the unconditional love of the divine consciousness. We become aware of what a child is in its essence because it is easy to see soul's consciousness in a baby, because it is so close to the surface of the skin on face (especially when it is sleeping); then we become aware of the omnipresence of life energy in everything, in existence itself, and that brings the activation of the fourth chakra. The same applies for any achievement; when we become aware of the essence of all human aspirations (third chakra), we become aware of the fact that they all are mere manifestations of the creative intelligence of the divine consciousness in existence.

When the third chakra is not connected with the fourth chakra, when it is closed and tied only to the lower chakras, then abnormal manifestations of power occur, together with all the worst goals - the dictatorship of single-mindedness, in man themselves, or in the family or society as a whole. The goals not based on understanding and love are generated here, and are justified with 'the end justifies the means', where the means are no longer chosen because there is no connection with the higher centers and soul's consciousness. Such people walk all over everyone, without mercy, on their path to their lower goals.

***

By connecting the first three chakras with the fourth, the functioning of the instinctive or motoric center is realized in a positive and creative way.

In order for the first three chakras to function properly, and to remain interconnected in a good way, it is necessary for them to be connected with the fourth chakra. Without this bond, their functioning is out of tune, which results in a twisted life. When they are connected with the fourth chakra, people enjoy the greatest happiness in both their private and social lives. When they are not connected with the fourth chakra, then life is very often based in suffering, for an individual and for society.

***

When the fourth chakra is successfully connected with the first three chakras, that is when the first three successfully connect and realize themselves in relation to the fourth; then the fourth chakra can connect with the fifth and successfully realize itself and all the lower chakras.

Connecting the fourth chakra with the fifth refers to expressing unconditional love and an emotional understanding of the nature of existence through thought, words and deeds. Our understanding does not mean much if we cannot express it. Love is not love if we do not express it. When we express it, we show the power of understanding. Expression is the characteristic of the fifth chakra. During expression all the weaknesses and all the virtues of our understanding are displayed, together with our emotional maturity.

***

Proper expression is not an option unless it is based on proper perception and insight. This means that the functioning of the fifth chakra, *vishuddhi*, is realized completely when it is connected with the sixth, ajna chakra. Perception is not right either, if it is not expressed.

***

Humans differ from all other beings in the fact that he possesses perception independent of space and time, of the type that surpasses sensory perception. Human perception is like this because it is not based on the body and physical senses, but on the pure soul's consciousness with which humans have contact through their higher mind, which is not in the body and therefore is not limited by sensory perception. The higher mind of humans is presented by the chakra *sahasrara*. To make sure that human perception is real and complete, the sixth chakra, ajna, must be connected with the seventh, *sahasrara*.

The only true perception and cognition man can receive from their higher mind connects him with the soul's consciousness. To the degree that perception and cognition do not come from the higher mind and soul's consciousness, perception and cognition are wrong. The cleaner and more straightforward our bond is with soul's consciousness, the truer and more complete our cognition.

***

The seventh chakra, *sahasrara*, is always connected with consciousness of the transcendental soul, with the divine consciousness that enables everything. It is placed above the head, which indicates that it is independent of the body and mind. It does not depend on anything. Practically this means that the divine consciousness is always with us, although we do not detect it due to our identification with the body and mind. The seventh chakra cannot be activated, but we can disrupt the functioning of the lower chakras and by doing so deprive ourselves of all the blessings of the seventh chakra. The seventh chakra actualizes itself with proper functioning of all the remaining chakras.

***

There is one general and very effective principle that sublimates consciousness and energy toward the psychoenergetic centers or chakras.

According to the testimony of people who have become aware of their existence between two lives via hypnotic regression, and those who had near death experiences they were for a fraction of time able to perceive their entire past life, and then had the ability to recapitulate everything they did - especially what they did to other people. At the same time they were able to experience how others felt about their actions toward them. They were able to experience their deeds both subjectively and objectively. This happens because of the holographic nature of existence; everything is One in the divine consciousness, everything is reflected in everything. Based on such an awareness, the soul decides when and where it will be born and continue its growth and correct its mistakes. This awareness of how the others experienced our actions is the key principle that leads us to maturity during the course of our lives. Its significance is so great that souls brought it into this world in their memory, and set it as the foundation of ethical principle, which says (do not) do unto others what you (do not) wish to be done unto yourself.

This fundamental principle of self-development works with the sublimating of consciousness through the chakras. If the negative functioning of some chakra relates to our conduct to other people (negativity always stops consciousness on a certain level and debases it to lower frequencies), then the objective consciousness of how others feel will pull us to a higher level, a higher chakra. When consciousness in us is mature enough and we begin to realize how others feel about our actions towards them, and they are in connection with some chakra or state of consciousness, then we automatically sublimate ourselves to higher understanding, to a higher chakra or higher state of consciousness.

The negative functioning refers to the first three chakras, the exchange of energy in its most elementary form (the first), by means of sexuality (the second) and willpower (the third chakra).

If the negative functioning of some chakra relates to activities that are in no way connected with other people, but with our personal habits and ways, the identical objective awareness toward ourselves will give us insight into how our being functions (as though our own deed is seen from the outside), and insight into the extent it stunts our karmic maturity in the context of our entire life. Indeed, when we look at a negative trait we possess in the context of our entire life and death, we surpass any attachment we may have to it.

The starting moment of maturity in objective awareness of oneself, and the malfunctioning of the lower chakras, Buddha described as: "There is too much disgust".

Objective awareness sublimates energy and existence into higher levels. Nothing else. Whenever we are objectively aware of something within us or outside of ourselves, we surpass it. The objective here means the opposite of subjective, or restricted in any way. Objective consciousness means awareness of objective reality.

The state of enlightenment, or samadhi, in the highest chakra, *sahasrara*, is the state of greatest objective awareness. It is the consciousness of our soul, which will persevere after physical life has ended, when we go back to our original, authentic state (*svarupa*). It is therefore called 'the great samadhi', or *maha-samadhi*. The purpose of our awareness is to possess consciousness of our soul, independent of the body and mind, before and after life in this world, to try and hold it during our lifetime, while we are still in this body and mind. Always. Because it is timeless.

It is achieved with the disappearance of all illusions we have about the body and mind, to think that we exist in space and time as separate entities, that we differ from the divine absolute who is everything that is.

SAMADHI
THE UNITY OF CONSCIOUSNESS AND EXISTENCE

According to the Biblical story God created the world in six days, and rested on the seventh. This story is actually about the chakras. Everything manifests itself through the seven chakras, and the seventh is the pure divine consciousness of itself. Six chakras represent all forms of existence, the seventh one is their transcendence. In the human experience transcendence is the most profound cognition, completely objective awareness, but unlike all other states of lower consciousness, transcendence is not based on any activity or the contents of the consciousness, it is the total surrender, which Buddha so adequately described as 'the ceasing' or 'extinction' (*nirvana*).

It is logical because the consciousness of unity is the consciousness of the quantum field from which and in which everything already exists timelessly. We experience here only individual manifestations of all the potentials of the quantum field in the illusion of space and time. The return into it is, therefore, possible only through surrender, the ceasing and extinction of all the illusions. This coming back is also an illusion because from this divine consciousness which is the whole we were never able to get out, it is everything and it is ourselves; it is the source of our consciousness. It is one more reason why you get into it with the surrender only. *Chan Buddhists* express these in words: when the mind is still the wrong viewpoints disappear all by themselves.

In order for the surrender to be possible it is necessary to overcome all the illusions; in order for the illusions to be overcome it takes the most powerful potential of pure consciousness combined with the highest potential of energy, that is the impact of consciousness.

The relation between consciousness and its effect (energy, *prana*) is depicted in the classical yoga as the two paths and their trajectory, the *ida* and *pingala*, that start at the first chakra, cross their paths and entwine around every single chakra on their way to the sixth chakra (*ajna*) where they join once again to enable the consciousness of unity of the seventh chakra. *Ida* and *pingala* actually represent the polarization of energy based on which it works. The polarization of energy is actually the polarization into the consciousness and action. The consciousness is non-Hertzian and action is the Hertzian frequency.

The entwining of trajectory of the consciousness and energy on its path around every chakra points to the fact that the the full awareness of the potential of every chakra is necessary, of every level of consciousness, of all the possible states and experiences of existence to balance the objective consciousness which is represented with the central trajectory, *sushumna*, which is between the *ida* and *pingala* and joins the first to the seventh chakra. *Sushumna* actually represents the balance of consciousness and energy, of *ida* and *pingala*, it connects the consciousness and existence with all the chakras, with all the states of consciousness, with all the possibilities of existence.[13]

---

[13] The identical idea is represented in the West with Hermes or Mercury's caduceus, as the symbol of science.

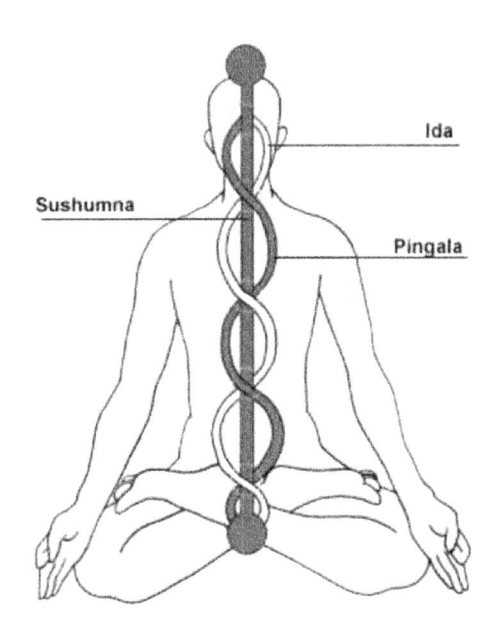

Therefore, it is very important to emphasize once more the significance of unity of consciousness and energy, the unity of thoughts and deeds, awareness and life. In the traditional graphic display of *ida* and *pingala*, it is clear that they cross and join in each chakra, which points to the merging of energy (being) and consciousness in each chakra. The joining of consciousness and energy activates each chakra in the proper way and sublimates us to the final awakening or realization, the seventh chakra.

Every chakra is unrealized only because of the lack of unity of consciousness and being (energy), because of their imbalance. The lack of unity and balance in our consciousness and actions, energy, consciousness and being, is the only factor that traps us in the lower states of existence, the only source of negativity and suffering. When it is pointed to positivity or towards the positive energy that sublimates us, the key factor is the unity of our deeds or energy with our consciousness, their balance and harmony. This unity is simply realized by doing whatever we are doing with our whole being, even the most trivial actions, in the here and now, and to be objectively aware of everything we do, as a witness. This is the non-Hertzian principle of consciousness. This principle, as the unity of energy and consciousness, of *ida* and *pingala*, in *sushumna*, was expressed in words long ago: "be what you are", "be here and now", and "awaken yourself".

The very presence of consciousness is a factor that harmonizes all oppositions. The very presence of consciousness has a natural tendency to become one with existence, because it is never completely separate from existence, as consciousness is the source of existence. Therefore, one should not do anything in order to realize the supreme alertness of the seventh chakra, apart from staying objective, unbiased and aware of every deed, as a witness. Being aware of the body and everything we do with the body, being aware of feelings and everything we feel, in any way we feel, being aware of expressing one's will or intention, and being aware of thoughts themselves. This means being aware of the functioning of all the chakras, all the states of consciousness, in all the dimensions we are comprised of and in which we exist. In this way consciousness itself is the factor that awakens us.

Enlightenment is nothing but enhancing consciousness. This is because existence is nothing but the emanation of consciousness itself. Together they realize and unite through their sheer presence. The only thing that should not be done is separating them. However, the illusion of this separation is what we experience as life, all the world that we see, all the suffering we go through. For that reason, it is said that life is just a dream, that the world is an illusion. What we mean by that is the world is an illusion if we perceive it as a collection of relative objects; but it is in fact real, as the absolute divine consciousness. Consciousness and existence are one, one absolute divine awareness of itself; it is all that there is and nothing else could be nor is even a possibility.

The illusion of their separation still takes place, though. Why? Because it is through this illusion that consciousness and existence exist as one, and in this way they experience absolutely all the potentials of existence and states of consciousness in their aspiration towards transcendence. Everything exists through transcendence, through surpassing; both consciousness and existence itself are nothing but one gigantic process of gradual surpassing. It is expressed through chakras in a manner where every single chakra expresses a lower or a higher state of consciousness and existence, in one act of supreme transcendence.

In the first chakra the divine consciousness exists, without the mind, in a minimal state of consciousness. It is pure existence, expressed through the form of minerals and the combination of elements.

In the second chakra the divine consciousness exists but in an unconscious state, like in a deep sleep without dreams, like in plants. It feels, but it does not have objective awareness of the nature of what it feels, or of itself as the subject of feelings. Plants feel everything, even our thoughts and feelings, but this does not help them develop any higher consciousness or sense; they only exist, and simply witness based on the rudimentary polarization of the experience of existence. Consciousness and existence begin to polarize here.

In the third chakra the divine consciousness realizes polarization in all possible ways, and that is why it can occasionally awaken and is aware of the nature of events; it can move and react, but is insufficiently aware of meaning, of the subject who is aware; it cannot comprehend and connect the role of the subject in objective phenomena, neither can it be inspired to creative work. This is the world of animals.

In the fourth chakra the divine consciousness, for the first time in existence, fully develops consciousness of the meaning of events, and of the subject who is aware. Actually, it is not possible to be objectively aware of the meaning of events without consciousness of the subject that is aware. Therefore, they always go together. The more they go hand in hand, the more we are objectively aware of ourselves as the subject in an objective chain of events and existence, and we can constructively affect further phenomena, and alter them to a certain degree with our creative endeavors. This is man, and the world of people. Here the first occasional awakening of the divine consciousness of itself takes place, awakening of transcendental awareness.

In the fifth chakra the divine consciousness acquires permanent experiences of the presence of its transcendental awareness in existence; or from the human perspective, man acquires permanent experience of their presence in the divine transcendental consciousness. This is enabled by expressing consciousness of the divine presence in existence (the fourth chakra), and by exchange of information of existence (the fifth chakra).

In the sixth chakra the divine consciousness, for the first time, directly expresses itself in existence. The divine consciousness, through *ajna* chakra, gives objective knowledge and perception to man. Complete perception of the manifested world is possible only through the complete perception of the subject who is aware of consciousness. Here, for the first time, the objective consciousness that enables existence itself recognizes itself as the consciousness of the subject, as self-consciousness.

In *ajna* chakra, consciousness that enables existence for the first time becomes an awareness of itself, through man. In *ajna* chakra, *ida* and *pingala* join completely, the energy and consciousness; existence is seen as conscious, and consciousness is experienced as a form of existence. And the reverse: a human's self-awareness (Self, *atman*) is in *ajna* the divine consciousness of itself that is aware of objective existence. This is called *savikalpa samadhi* in Patanjali's science of yoga, or the consciousness of unity which is not completely clean, but which is seasoned with 'the seed' of experience of existence. When consciousness of itself becomes pure - meaning perfect - it becomes transcendental, *nirvikalpa samadhi*, completely independent of the experience of existence, untainted by the illusion of existence.

We have stated that existence itself rests on consciousness, that existence is in its essence the divine consciousness itself, with an awareness of itself. In the pure awareness of itself, in the seventh chakra, *sahasrara*, there are no illusions of existence, no projections. From its perspective every form of existence is a fall of the consciousness into some form of illusion of existence. Every chakra below sahasrara represents an even greater degree of polarization, a greater loss of awareness of oneself, a greater loss of the absolute balance of opposites, down to the lowest chakra, where the principle of opposites exists all by itself as the principle of pure energy.

In the first chakra, the pure energy of existence is present; existence itself is pure energy. In the seventh chakra the pure consciousness of existence is present; more precisely, existence is pure consciousness. All the chakras are the process of their uniting and separating -

the act of understanding all possible states of consciousness and existence.

The first chakra is the furthest Hertzian state, and the seventh chakra is the furthest non-Hertzian state.

In order for existence to realize itself completely, consciousness should crystallize in existence in its original non-Hertzian condition; pure awareness of oneself should be united with all possible experiences of existence, and with all the potentials of existence. The science of tantra and alchemy have done this since antiquity, with more or less success. From this esoteric science, the exoteric science which is known to us today originated, and built this civilization. All material culture and science are nothing but a reflection of uniting consciousness and existence through man; more accurately, it is human ability to unite consciousness and energy, work and action in this world. All of human evolution and history are based on this.

Human evolution and history finalize and realize in samadhi, in the unity of consciousness and existence. Humans begin to exist in a corporeal form as the consciousness of the divine soul in all shapes and possibilities of existence.

Earlier, soul's consciousness was losing itself due to identification with many existing life forms, which were stronger than it. Every lower chakra was a point of 'decline' of soul's consciousness into lower forms, and greater identification with existence. These were simply ways for the divine consciousness to become aware of all the potentials of existence, of itself. When it is 'returned' to itself, to its original state in the seventh chakra, in samadhi, to its full potential, then it will be able to move through all the possibilities of existence, through all the other chakras, without losing awareness of itself.

The entire process is this: the divine consciousness of itself, to be present in its highest potential and purity, and effective in all potential forms of existence, in all states of being, without identification, independent, through man, as a human's soul's consciousness – without the loss of its original potential.

This process takes place in three steps.

Our experience of existence was, in the beginning, the oblivion of our true nature, the soul's consciousness, the sole experience of the Hertzian frequency of the physical world, with all the restrictions of perception and the power to act. It is this life that is known to all of us in this world. The ***first step*** in the process of self-knowing was for the real nature of the physical world to be known (*sat*, the being, existence); that it is nothing all by itself and unto itself, but is merely a reflection or projection of the universal field of existence, the quantum field, *akasha*, by which the absolute divine consciousness keeps manifesting itself. The first step consists of recognition of the mind, from proper understanding of the nature of reality.

When this cognition matures to a sufficient degree, so it is no longer an occasional but a permanent reality, it then includes the entire being and its actions; more precisely, the awareness of reality includes energy, too, and actions taking place in that reality. In the first step we only occasionally recognize the reality of consciousness and existence, the reality of the divine Absolute. It is called *savikalpa samadhi* – samadhi, which is mixed with impressions of the manifested world.

When consciousness of reality and energy with which we live are joined, the ***second step*** occurs in which the objective, material world disappears and pure consciousness (*chit*) is uncovered as the essence of existence itself, and this consciousness is discovered as our self-consciousness, as its essence (Self, *atman*). In the first moments of such cognition, an awakened man is not able to participate in the physical world, because it is revealed as a dream for the awakened one. The awakened one is unable to participate in these dreams any longer. They are independent of existence. All the states of consciousness, daylight living, sleep, deep sleep without dreams, change before their eyes as though they are witnesses. They cannot be identified with any objects, but only with the subject, with themselves, with the pure consciousness that enables everything, with the divine consciousness; they can never lose consciousness of themselves, to be something that they are not, because they always see existence itself as a reflection of the divine consciousness.

Such experience Buddha expressed with the words: 'it is not me, it is not mine' - regarding the body, mind, ego, and all the states of consciousness. This state is also expressed in descriptions of the world as an illusion or dream. The second step is, practically speaking, the permanent realization of transcendence, the nature of consciousness of the divine Absolute. It is called *nirvikalpa samadhi* – samadhi, without any illusions regarding the manifested world.

This original authenticity and independence of consciousness from any identification with being or existence, is called *kaivalya* in Patanjali's science of yoga. The word *kaivalya* marks the state of what is simple, unmixed with anything, authentic, pure, and therefore contains the idea of perfection and completion. All of this is based on the idea of separation, surpassing, or transcendence. Perfection and authenticity of human consciousness and essence are not possible without transcendence, without surpassing the body and mind. It is manifested by the space between the seventh chakra and the body, as it is a little above the top of the head. This space means that it cannot be reached with anything which comes from the body and mind, and through no effort or process. It is only achieved by surrender through self-awareness of all other states of consciousness (by actualizing the other six chakras).

The seventh chakra (or *nirvikalpa samadhi*) is actualized in two ways only: either by surrender or by self-cognition. Self-cognition is the path of meditation and discipline of mental stillness, the direct transcendence of the mind. It is realized in the practice of Buddhist meditation (*dhyana, vipassana, satipatthana, zazen, shikan taza*; for details of the practice of meditation, see my book "*Meditation - The First and Last Step*"). Meditation works so that when our body and mind completely calm down, nothing can happen but an opening up to what is beyond the body and mind, the consciousness of the higher mind, the soul's consciousness, the consciousness of the universal quantum field that enables everything and that is everything, irrelevant of space and time.

When we stop blurring it together, it manifests itself. The body and mind cannot be quieted by force, but only through a very subtle realization that we are neither our body nor mind; by surpassing the identification with the body and mind, which is the basis of ignorance (metaphysical and any other). All the motions and phenomena of the body and mind fall under the category of Hertzian frequencies. Stillness has the non-Hertzian frequency of the quantum field. That is the technique of meditation. There must be no ideological or religious content (those are all traces of the Hertzian frequencies of the mind) and as such, are objective and void of all content, like Patanjali and Buddhist meditation recommended here.

The experience of meditation directly manifests the unity of consciousness and existence. When we quieten the mind in meditation, we reach consciousness which is beyond the mind and its contents; when we become just a witness, we become existence itself. In the pure, transcendental consciousness of ourselves we do not differ from pure existence, timeless presence, here and now.

Therefore, it is of crucial importance that meditation is tied to neither metaphysical, ideological or religious beliefs, and especially not the mental contents of a personal nature, because it is in its essence the type of practice in which existence expresses itself directly as consciousness, and consciousness as existence. Therefore, real meditation is nothing but a cleansing and release of such contents - mental hygiene.

Self-knowing is a direct path, and it is suitable only for those mature souls who are finalizing their cycle of incarnations, which means that they are not attached to the manifested world. Surrender is more accessible to those who still take part in the experience of the world, but for that reason it is combined with the risks of mixing the contents of the mind, which can be very subtle; and then the whole affair turns into a pseudo religious performance and an act of self-deception. Surrender in its essence means complete understanding and acceptance that we are neither our body, nor our mind, but the transcendental soul's consciousness which surpasses and enables, in accordance with knowledge and experience of the nature of consciousness and existence. The same is experienced in meditation. This means that self-knowing and surrender have the same final act: they merge into one. Self-knowing cannot be realized without complete surrendering, nor can surrender be realized without complete self-knowing.

Surrender and final self-cognition can be understood only by understanding the nature of the frequency of the first and the seventh chakra, using the analogy of mirrors.

We have already stated that the nature of the frequencies of the first and the seventh chakras are opposite: Hertzian and non-Hertzian. These two frequencies interact as mirrors; more precisely, as opposites, or a reverse image of the reflected. Everything that appears in the rough reality of the three-dimensional world (the first three chakras) to be in linear time and separate in space is playing out gradually under the influence of the cause, and the same thing applies to the non-Hertzian frequency of the universal quantum field (seventh chakra), where the timeless presence is already ever present and realized, complete and perfect. The Hertzian mirror is nature, in which all of existence in linear space and time is played out. The divine consciousness of our soul originates from the non-Hertzian universal quantum field. It is only an illusory difference that exists due to the difference in frequencies. This simulacrum is the essence of all illusions and ignorance in which man lives, unless they have made an effort to actualize the chakras. It is the cause for all our incarnations and life dramas. Awakening from that illusion, distracting attention (of consciousness) from the reverse state of affairs (the image in the mirror -existence), is the purpose and goal of all our lives.

When consciousness and energy get together in *ajna* chakra, they have come as close as possible to the non-Hertzian frequency field where things become reversed. That is why we are then able to see with *ajna* chakra, or 'the third eye', the real nature of things; we see that everything is timeless, and we are able to be psychic only because everything is already present in the non-Hertzian quantum field, there is no time during which everything is realized, as they are already there; there is not even space as an idea of separation. Everything is already present and achieved in the non-Hertzian quantum field, and for that reason a psychic person can see all of this, because they have contact with this field in which everything already is. He can only see what the linear mind attached to the body, and the Hertzian frequencies of the lower chakras are able to transcend.

We can see reality only to the point we do not resist it – because in the absolute sense it already is. When we imagine reality being something other than it already is, here and now, we resist it, **and what we keep resisting gains momentum against us; this phenomena of resisting reality is the only shackle that perpetuates our illusion, ignorance and suffering, and we add to its power.** Therefore, the physical reality we do not like, but are forced to live in, has been brought about by our resistance to the reality of our soul, the divine reality which is always here and now and in everything. The cessation of resistance to reality, whatever it may be, is the starting point of its creative change. The first and the last step is always surrendering and acceptance. Basically, contrary to everything that keeps our Hertzian mind trapped in the illusion of time, and the way it presents it to itself.

This experience, in other systems of self-development, was described as seeing the Unity, everything within oneself and oneself in everything. All other powers or siddhi are merely a manifestation of the non-Hertzian frequency of consciousness in the field of

Hertzian existence, or the quantum mind in the physical world.

One further point must be emphasized here: soul's consciousness, or the quantum mind, the non-Hertzian frequencies, can be manifested in the physical world of Hertzian frequencies, but the reverse is impossible. Nothing that possesses Hertzian frequency, which appears to be separate in time and space, can exist in the non-Hertzian reality of the divine Absolute, in the consciousness of our soul. It can also be said that a mirror can exist in the world, but the reverse reflection, the picture of the world from the mirror, can never be real in the world.

With this we have reached the final **third step** in the process of our existence and awakening. It is the surpassing of all the differences between the Hertzian and the non-Hertzian frequencies of existence in unity. It is the true unity of consciousness and existence. They together constitute reality, the divine absolute reality, which is manifested through the prism of the seven states of consciousness or chakras, and the purest is in the highest, seventh chakra, the purest consciousness a man can have of themselves. This consciousness is not of this world. An awakened individual lives in this world as though they are not of this world, but he lives their life to the fullest, with in the first moments of such cognition, an awakened man is not able to participate in the physical world, because it is revealed as a dream for the awakened one. The awakened one is unable to participate in these dreams any longer maximum energy and awareness, because he sees that nothing is wrong or different from the most supreme divine reality.

In order to realize consciousness of their soul while still in the body and mind, he cannot identify with the body or mind. He must first realize transcendence. The same is true of dreaming and awakening. He cannot be in both states at the same time. With the awakening of our soul, all the dreams of the manifested world disappear, dreams of space and time in which our divine existence was not the one that is. However, a true knowledge of illusion and surpassing it is in the knowledge that it was never real. As long as we keep trying to get rid of an illusion, we give it reality, which it itself never had.

All the previous states were some form of reaction. Even *nirvikalpa samadhi* was a reaction to the *savikalpa samadhi*, in the same way that *savikalpa samadhi* was a reaction to the state of ignorance and unconsciousness of the mundane mind. This final third step is called *sahaja samadhi* - the natural, permanent or infinite samadhi, which is not a reaction to anything, which is outside all opposites, even existence and non-existence, consciousness and unconsciousness.

Now is the time to say that only our "I" was part of the illusion, it does not exist outside of our I (ego). Our individual I is the only factor in every illusion. Our I, our individual mind, was the only factor which made the difference between the Hertzian and the non-Hertzian frequencies, with all the consequences to the world; or more accurately put, to our perception of the world. Awakening of man is nothing but the surpassing of all the limitations of the individual mind or its I (ego). With this, all illusions are overcome.

Only then are we complete in the consciousness of our soul, in the divine consciousness which is everything, in the *sahaja samadhi*. The final *sahaja samadhi* is the presence of the most supreme consciousness of our soul in the physical body, which never happens naturally of its own accord; the kind of soul's consciousness which is so high and pure that it always stays unembodied, above even the higher mind. It does not descend into the body following a natural process, at the moment of birth of the body, it is only able to descend into the body once man has done everything regarding their awareness and awakening, so that nothing else remains, when he finishes the karmic learning cycle, incarnations. Completing the cycle of incarnations (the ceasing of being born over and over again, of ignorance and suffering) is nothing but the complete cognition of consciousness of the pure soul, which never incarnates. Expressions like 'enlightenment', 'knowing God' or 'knowing oneself' (the Self, *Atman*) do not designate anything but cognition of consciousness of one's soul, which existed before birth in this body and will exist after this body; the cognition of its absolute nature, while we still are in this body, in this world.

When we die we bitterly regret, after the death of the body, that we did not awaken the immortal divine consciousness of our soul, which we always are in our essence, and instead used that incarnation to live spellbound by the trivial contents of our physical mind, induced by an illusion of individual separation, by identification with the physical body, and suffered as a result of that. We always kept promising ourselves that next time we would live to express better the consciousness of our soul, to remember ourselves, our true nature, and in that state the seeming greatest separation from the divine essence, which life in this physical world represents, and that we would resist the alluring attraction of the contents of the mind and always stay aware of consciousness itself and its source, the source of all existence. We are always coming into this world with this motive in mind, and due to the greatness of this undertaking, the greatness that shaped all life on this planet, it takes many attempts for us to finally succeed in our mission. The state of *sahaja samadhi* is the state of the soul that has achieved this goal.

The consciousness of our soul would not be what it is if anything else existed other than itself. Nothing else but consciousness of our soul itself can exist, our individuality included. Therefore, its authentic state cannot be a reaction to anything that would be non-authentic. The divine absolute is the only reality. The entire process of our existence is merely an attempt to recognize this reality in ourselves, and in everything else, as existence itself. To know ourselves as the divine reality. We are simply going from one life into another, because we see in the divine reality some difference, something other than itself – the difference between 'this' and 'that' world, life and death, the awakened state and dreaming, right and wrong. We see it like this in order to have a motive to experience everything. In the most supreme reality, there is no difference, nor is there anything that is not it itself. In the language of the mind we say that it is nothing, for this exact reason, we refer to nothing else, nothing it is not. Everything within it is perfect, the way it is, because it is everything that is happening.

Humans in *sahaja samadhi*, in full awareness of the soul's consciousness, live completely aware of their past lives, the ones they have before this physical birth, which is logical because soul's consciousness is a witness to all of them. Getting to know one's previous lives means getting acquainted with their meaning and value; they all happened so that we could get to know the consciousness of our soul in all the possibilities of existence. That is why this life is loved and revered the most, every moment and in every respect, because it is the outcome of all our previous lives, and it is a reflection of the soul's consciousness.

That is why, for the human in *sahaja samadhi*, nothing exists except the divine reality; they have not the slightest idea that they were ever born. It is so because now they have the soul's consciousness which was not born in any one body - the body is just a dream. The conviction that we were born is the cornerstone of every illusion, and of death also. It is impossible for him to be identified with the body in any way, because he always sees the wholeness of the divine presence. They do not see their body as their own, they see it in complete harmony with the earth, the sky, and the entire cosmos, with the entirety. They do not see themselves as being born in a body but in the physical universe. They see clearly that their whole body is the whole physical universe, which is in its basic, subatomic, quantum level, completely interconnected into one unique being.

In reality there is nothing separate in all the physical world; therefore, no physical body is separate and different from the rest of the universe. The body is merely a favourable place and a reference point from which it can be involved in the drama of experiencing all the possibilities of existence in the physical universe. Nothing else. That is why he sees clearly that the consciousness of their soul has never been born in one body, but in the physical universe, and the body is merely a good spot from which to gather experiences of existence, a reference point which moves through the three-dimensional experience of existence – and the experience of existence appears three-dimensional in linear time only because it is observed from one reference point, from the physical body. No other reason.

They are independent of any form of existence. That is why they have a completely objective awareness of every form of existence.

To humans, life and death are equally illusory. One who sees this difference moves from life to life and gives importance to the former at the expense of the latter.

They live in the present moment as though it is the last in this world, as though they were already dead, but for that exact reason every moment is ecstasy. The full potential of life, in every moment, can be experienced only from the perspective that surpasses life.

They do not make known the fact that they are more aware than other people, because in all people, even in their unconsciousness, they see the impact of the consciousness of the divine Absolute. Nothing exists for the human that is not the divine consciousness; dreams, illusions and stupidity are all expressions of the divine consciousness, as the most supreme wisdom. This is because humans does not distinguish the divine consciousness from existence itself.

They do not see a difference between sleeping and functioning in everyday activities, and still they find their way perfectly, both in sleep and in awakened functioning - and apparently much better than those who identify with the contents of their dreams, in sleep and during the day.

Nothing exists that is wrong for him, because nothing can be outside the divine Absolute, yet he always acts, speaks and thinks properly, because the divine consciousness is never different from themselves. For him it is impossible to be incorrect.

To them everything is equally real, because they are independent of everything. They know that the greatest human value begins where individuality stops. They never seek safety in the body, because they know the body is just a consequence of a higher cause, a far bigger power, the soul's consciousness. They have sanctuary in the cause of all things.[14] They do not possess their I (ego) because they are not separate from the divine consciousness that is everything; nonetheless, they act as a perfect, complete person, which is the personification of the presence of the perfect and complete divine consciousness. Within themselves they are always the same, although they enjoy any outer change or difference. They can do so only because they have within them the consciousness of the supreme soul which is above birth and existence itself. They live inconspicuously among other humans as workers, poets, both princes and paupers; others do not notice them for the same reason they do not notice the permanent presence of the consciousness of the divine Absolute in everything, every moment of every day. For the same reason, they have no need to disclose themselves to anyone. They cannot partake in their dreams. In order for others to recognize them, they must first recognize the consciousness of the divine Absolute in themselves.

These are to name but a few traits of the full potential of the unborn soul's consciousness, once it finds itself in the body, which is called *sahaja samadhi*.

These three steps are described in Shankara's advaita vedanta with the expression *sat-cit-ananda*. *Sat* is being or existence, *cit* is the pure transcendental consciousness, *ananda* is the supreme bliss found in us once we become aware of their unity.

There is no existence (*sat*) without consciousness (*cit*). Consciousness is manifested as existence, as every-

---

[14] The gospel of John: 12:24-25.

thing that is. Recognizing the unity of consciousness and existence only happens in man, completely, as heavenly bliss, *ananda* ('kingdom come'), a timeless and ever present unconditional divine love, both in man and in everything that exists, and in everything that takes place. If it were not already in everything, as the true nature of everything, a man could not experience it.

When people become aware of their true origin, which enables their existence, they will create heaven on earth. It is the simplest definition of uniting consciousness and existence.

Humans are merely conscious subjects in which consciousness and existence coalesce. Only once consciousness and existence join perfectly in humans and recognize one another in unity - a unity that is expressed through humans as unconditional divine love. The divine Absolute itself expresses its unconditional love through man.

All of life and nature were designed to this end.

Printed in Great Britain
by Amazon